## Praise for *Becoming Kin: An Indigenous Call to Unforgetting the Past and Reimagining Our Future*

"An invitation and a challenge to become better relatives to one another at this critical moment in human and planetary history. Generous and wise, *Becoming Kin* is a rare book designed to be put to immediate and practical use."

—Naomi Klein, *New York Times*–bestselling author and professor of climate justice at the University of British Columbia

"*Becoming Kin* is a powerful invitation into unlearning and learning. Krawec offers an essential vision for our relationships with the earth, the land, and each other."

—Rabbi Danya Ruttenberg, author of *On Repentance and Repair: Making Amends in an Unapologetic World*

"A must-read for those working toward understanding and dismantling colonization. Patty Krawec reminds us what it means to come home to ourselves, this earth, and one another, and invites us to ask the beautiful, difficult questions that will help us reclaim that belonging."

—Kaitlin Curtice, author of *Native: Identity, Belonging, and Rediscovering God*

"Krawec holds space for Indigenous kin in a broad sense—and Black displanted people—and offers us a needed treatise on how to think.

I will be reading and rereading this book for years to come, and I know it will inform my work as a Black feminist scientist."

—Chanda Prescod-Weinstein, author of
*The Disordered Cosmos: A Journey into Dark Matter,
Spacetime, and Dreams Deferred*

"Generous but also demanding, in the best way possible. A wonderful expression of how we can become better kin, with the world and with ourselves."

—Jesse Wente, author of *Unreconciled: Family, Truth,
and Indigenous Resistance*, arts journalist,
and director of Canada's Indigenous Screen Office

"Patty Krawec has written a passionate and profound meditation on lineage, community, and systemic erasure. Grand in scope and depth of research, yet intimate in the telling, this book is an education for the soul."

—Omar El Akkad, Giller Prize–winning author of
*What Strange Paradise* and *American War*

"Crucial for understanding both colonization and Indigeneity, *Becoming Kin* is part history, part memoir, and part inspiration, lighting a path forward based on successful race relations, peace, and understanding."

—Keri Leigh Merritt, historian and writer

"*Becoming Kin* is stunning; both in its indictment of colonial violence and especially in its painstakingly brilliant and beautiful articulation of another world and the reorganization of our relations beyond the nation-state, colonialism, and oppression. This book is a rigorous yet generous invitation to learn, to imagine, to dream, to act—to *become* kin."

—Harsha Walia, author of *Border and Rule: Global Migration, Capitalism, and the Rise of Racist Nationalism* and *Undoing Border Imperialism*

"Our interconnectedness with nature—and each other—is central to Indigenous teachings. Patty Krawec draws from Indigenous wisdom, history, and personal insight to reveal a path forward. Incisive and beautifully written, this book is a vital guide to coming together in greater kinship."

—Ziya Tong, science broadcaster and author of *The Reality Bubble: Blind Spots, Hidden Truths and the Dangerous Illusions That Shape Our World*

"*Becoming Kin* is a brilliant work of critical analysis woven into a tapestry of autobiographical reflections. Krawec deconstructs settler colonialism through a personal lens and invites readers to travel with her on a journey of myth, reflection, and healing."

—Lee Francis IV, CEO and publisher of Red Planet Books and Comics

"*Becoming Kin* speaks powerful truths about our collective histories of violence; it not only encourages but also provides next steps for us to do better, now that we know better."

—Dr. Robyn Bourgeois, acting vice provost for Indigenous engagement, Brock University

"A brilliant, generous book—a must-read for anyone who wants to show up for a world of possibility rather than doom. Patty Krawec beckons us into perceiving our interconnections, with a powerful recentering of how we tell stories and histories for transformed futures."

—Alexis Shotwell, author of *Against Purity: Living Ethically in Compromised Times*

"*Becoming Kin* is an act of hospitality. Krawec is a compelling story-teller, and this book is a powerful offering of hope and redemption in the journey of becoming kin."

—Michael Krause, teaching pastor at Southridge Community

# BECOMING KIN

# BECOMING KIN

An Indigenous Call to Unforgetting
the Past and Reimagining Our Future

PATTY KRAWEC

BROADLEAF BOOKS
MINNEAPOLIS

BECOMING KIN
An Indigenous Call to Unforgetting the Past and Reimagining Our Future

Excerpt from "graduate school first semester: so here I am writing about Indians again" from *Mother/Land* by Cheryl Savageau (Cromer, UK: Salt Publishing, 2006). Reprinted by permission of author.

Excerpt from "Orphans of God" by Mark Heard, 1992, Satellite Sky. Reprinted with permission by Janet Heard.

Cover image: beadwork by Giniw Paradis; photography by Jenessa Galenkamp
Cover design: 1517 Media

Print ISBN: 978-1-5064-7825-8
eBook ISBN: 978-1-5064-7826-5

*stop writing about Indians*
*she told me again*
*only louder as if*
*I was hard of hearing*
*you have to allow authors*
*their subjects, she said*
*stop writing about*
*what isn't in the text*
*which is just our entire history*

—Cheryl Savageau



*We are soot-covered urchins running wild and unshod*
*We will always be remembered as the orphans of God*
*They will dig up these ruins and make flutes of our bones*
*And blow a hymn to the memory of the orphans of God*

—Mark Heard

# CONTENTS

# FOREWORD

Our present reality is a cacophony of suffering and despair. A virus tears through the most vulnerable among us, taking the elderly and those made precarious by neglect and abandonment. The planet burns as billionaires rake in record profits at the height of a global pandemic. Levels of inequality rise alongside temperatures and sea levels. Life expectancies drop as the death conditions—which have always defined a for-profit global system of plunder—intensify.

Moreover, the cacophony of suffering is met by equally rapturous protest. Tens of millions shouted against the death worlds with an affirmative and simple phrase: Black Lives Matter. Water Protectors quieted the sounds of grinding metal tearing into the earth by attaching themselves to heavy machinery to halt the construction of oil pipelines. Time seems to standstill in these brief moments of rupture.

In these pages, Patty Krawec, an Anishinaabekwe, meditates on those moments of calm, which seem always on the brink of being entirely consumed by a terrible danger. It is the moment a Water Protector locks down pipeline equipment, silencing the guns and money people with a humble prayer, even if for a moment. It is the moment humble people try to make sense of why another brother, sister, mother, relative, river, mountain, and life is needlessly destroyed or stolen.

A world of bad relations—what in Lakota could be called owasicu owe, or "the way of the fat-taker"—is what has brought us to this point. What better symbolizes the cynicism of this mentality than the richest people on this planet trying to escape it in a billionaire-funded space race? The for-profit system commodified our other-than-human relations. They were made into "nature" or "natural resources" to be boundlessly exploited and consumed. Humanity itself was transformed into a mass of laborers and consumers, working for bosses. Bad relations are making our earth uninhabitable while simultaneously being elevated to the level of the cosmos.

"Grief is the persistence of love," Krawec writes. Indeed. Grief and love are not bound by time and space. In Indigenous worlds, Land Defenders act out of necessity and survival, protecting rivers and landscapes from destruction. They do so out of mourning for a world taken from them through centuries of colonialism. But they also do so out of love and solidarity for life that currently exists and life that has yet to be created on this planet. They are ancestors of the future, motivated by grief as the persistence of love.

Grief is also about remembering, or unforgetting, the future and a history that could have been. We were first colonized when they took away our collective sense of a future. The evidence of that crime lies in church and government lands interred with the remains of Native children, the evidence of a future they tried to snuff out.

As Lakota people, we recognize becoming human is hard. It is marked by terrible suffering and profound beauty, especially in an age of cacophony and chaos. But at the center of making relations is love, ceremony, song, laughter, and crying. The quiet persistence of love. Therefore, Krawec's vision is bold. She takes us on a journey of becoming human by first understanding how we relate to each other, our history, and—hopefully—our collective future.

It begins by listening.

—*Nick Estes (Lower Brule Sioux Tribe) is a historian and author of* Our History Is the Future, Standing with Standing Rock, *and* Red Nation Rising

# NII'KINAAGANAA

**W**e are related. Nii'kinaaganaa.

My friend Josh Manitowabi breaks down this Anishinaabe word like this. *Nii*: "I am" or "my." *Kinaa*: "all of them." *Ganaa*: "relatives, my relatives." The phrase could mean any of these things: I am my relatives, all of them. I am related to everything. All my relations.

From our earliest creation stories, the Anishinaabeg (plural of *Anishinaabe*) understood themselves to be related not only to each other but to all of creation. Our language does not divide into male and female the way European languages do. It divides into animate and inanimate. The world is alive with beings that are other than human, and we are all related, with responsibilities to each other.

This concept of relatedness is by no means unique to the Anishinaabeg. After the Standing Rock pipeline protests, the Lakota phrase mitakuye oyasin became well known outside of Lakota communities. But it came to mean something less than what it means to the Lakota. Many people think it means "all my relations," and it does, but it also means much more than that. It is specific to the Lakota people and their thinking in a way that can't be fully translated. Similarly, nii'kinaaganaa means "we are related"—and also more than that.

For years, I belonged to a mailing list that named itself for the song in the second epigraph. We thought it was a lovely, poetic image for those of us who felt outside of the traditional church, but then we dug down into the lyrics and discovered Heard wasn't talking about us as a small group of disaffected Christians. He was talking broadly about us as the American church—how the church is a pale shadow of what it could have been, should have been. The dominant church is running wild and unshod over this beautiful earth, with no regard for anyone else. A people who, despite grasping for power, have become ruins and hollow bones. Western Christians have, as they say, lost the plot. Throughout this book, we will trace that loss, that forgetting, and in reclaiming history, we will unforget the things we used to know.

The Americas—the countries of the United States and Canada, Mexico, Brazil, and others on these western continents—have a creation story too. It is an emerging creation story that has the power to determine who Americans are and who we can be.

We need to unforget our histories and the relationships they contain. We need to become kin.

Nii'kinaaganaa.

Language is complicated.

Through my father, I am Ojibwe Anishinaabe. The Ojibwe live mainly around the Great Lakes, in what is now known as Ontario, Manitoba, Minnesota, North Dakota, Wisconsin, and Michigan. The Anishinaabeg are a large group and cover a huge geography, with many subgroups that include the Chippewa, Michi Saagig, Odawa, Saulteaux, Ojibwe, Potawatomi, Nipissing and Algonquin. These aren't interchangeable. We are all Anishinaabe, but there are some linguistic and cultural differences among the groups.

Anishinaabe simply means "the people," and this type of self-naming is common throughout the Americas. We identify ourselves as "the people" and then describe those who are different from us according to our relationship with them. This has had some unfortunate consequences. For example, the Haudenosaunee and the Lakota are societies with whom the Anishinaabe have had historically conflicted relationships. So when the French colonists asked their Anishinaabe allies about other tribal groups, we told them what *we* called them rather than their own names for themselves. *Iroquois* may be more familiar to you than *Haudenosaunee*, *Sioux* more familiar than *Lakota*. But the former terms are French versions of Wendat and Anishinaabe words meaning something like "snakes."

We are all related, but clearly we don't always get along.

The people who are indigenous to the Western Hemisphere have been called so many things. To Columbus and many who came after, we are *Indians*, which is still a legal category in the United States and Canada. We have also been described as *red* in an attempt to fit us into a color-coded racial hierarchy, a designation most commonly associated with a particular slur that, until recently, named a national football team. *Native Americans* and *Native Canadians* tend to be more common. For a brief time in Canada, we were called *Aboriginal*. But the prefix *ab-* actually means "not," so the word means that we aren't original to this place—you can understand why we would object to that. And of course, *Indigenous* is not unique to the Western Hemisphere; there are Indigenous peoples across the globe. In this book, I'll use all these terms for reasons that mostly make sense to me; there are times when a particular term just feels more correct to the context, but that is entirely subjective.

In the United States, people generally talk about Native Americans, Hawai'ians, and Alaska Natives. In Canada, people will

frequently refer to First Nations, Inuit, and Métis. The Inuit are a cir-
cumpolar people, along with the Sámi of Scandinavia and the Aleut
and Yupik of the United States and Russia, as well as many others
who live in the Arctic regions. The Métis are a distinct people who
emerged after contact in western Canada and the northern United
States just as the Lumbee, Comanche, Seminole, and Oji-Cree
emerged elsewhere after colonization, distinct cultures tied to land
and ancestors. *First Nations* can refer broadly to the original peoples
but most often refers to reserve communities and not nations at all.
Anishinaabe is a nation; Lac Seul First Nation, where my father,
myself, and my children are registered as Indians, is a reserve.

Clear as mud? I hope that this will make more sense as we go
along. Each of these terms is correct and wrong, and it is likely that
whatever term you use will at some point be corrected by somebody
else to a term they think is more appropriate. The best thing to do
is thank them for the correction and move on, recognizing that language is complicated. These terms were rarely what we called ourselves and represent colonial ways of thinking about us. And so they
will all be wrong in some way.

If there are some who are Indigenous, there are some who are not,
and most of those who are not are settlers. *Settlers*: this word is just
as fraught as any word for Indigenous peoples is, and it also refers
to a collective group. You may be more inclined to think of yourself as American or Canadian. Perhaps being called a "settler" feels
aggressive—a suggestion that you do not belong, despite generations
of being here. You think of yourself, or perhaps your ancestors, as
immigrants. Not settlers. Settlers are not immigrants. Immigrants
come to a place and become part of the existing political system.
When the colonists arrived in what would become the Americas,
there were many political systems already in existence. Ours. And

although the Haudenosaunee system likely inspired or shaped the US system of governance, there has never been a time when those who came to these shores collectively became part of any of our political systems. (Exceptions may include those who became the Métis, the Lumbee, and the Seminole.) Settler is a way of *being* here. Through this book, I hope to offer you another way to be.

Black people are not settlers—not those who are descended from the ones who came in chains, nor those who came afterward— because Blackness envelops them all and holds them distinct from other migrants. There are some words gaining ground to describe Black relationship to this place: arrivants, displanted. I like the term *displanted*, a word coined by an African Canadian human rights lawyer, because it describes the violence of this movement as well as one's ability to put down roots again and again. And of course, Black and Indigenous are not mutually exclusive categories. In many places where colonialism touched down, it is Black people who are Indigenous, and throughout the Americas, many Indigenous people are also Black. We did not only intermarry with Europeans, after all. So when I talk about Black and Indigenous people, know that I am talking about broad, overlapping communities. Discrete categories make for a convenient shorthand, but they rarely do justice to the people involved.

A small note about the Anishinaabe language that is scattered throughout the book: I am not fluent in the Anishinaabe language— far from it—but at times I find it helpful to reflect on particular Anishinaabe words. They prompt me to shift my thinking. The words are pronounced phonetically, and when I use them, I will provide you with a general translation. But I use the Anishinaabe word also to remind you that it means more than that. As with any translation, there is not a simple exchange of one word for another; there are concepts about place and relationship that go along with these words. I want these words to prompt you to shift your thinking, to root our thinking in the place where they were born, a place the Anishinaabe and many others know as Turtle Island, what is currently known as North America.

As we begin this work—and it will be work—I hope that you have somebody to do it with you. I hope somebody else is reading this alongside you so that you can talk about the things you are learning and being asked to do.

Aambe: let's go.

# INTRODUCTION

I wait at the back of the stage, behind the curtains, holding my hand drum and listening to the low buzz of a theater filled with people. My friend Karl stands in the darkness at center stage, waiting for me to start singing and make my way to where he stands. We are providing an opening for the Niagara Performing Arts Center's season preview. It is not a Native event. The center is a public arts venue that showcases a wide range of performers, and the artistic directors include Native artists throughout the regular season. They have asked Karl and me to open this particular night as an acknowledgment that this and future events take place on Haudenosaunee and Anishinaabe land.

It is the fall of 2017, 150 years since Canada's confederation, and I've made a ribbon skirt to wear at this event. Ribbon skirts—long cotton skirts embellished with rows of ribbon and sometimes with appliqued designs—are a contemporary innovation of an older style of clothing that we wore before settler contact. The ribbon skirt I've made for this evening is black with wide ribbons in the colors associated with the medicine wheel: red, black, white, and yellow. I have appliqued red maple leaves falling down the front of the skirt until they are covered by ribbons. I like the imagery of Canada being absorbed by Indigenous ideas. Later, during the gathering after the event, a couple of women will come to speak with me. They will comment that the leaves are upside down. A nation in distress flies their flag upside down, I will tell them. And Canada, like the United States, is a nation in distress.

It occurs to me in that moment, as I wait backstage, how much has changed in my life. Like many Native people born between 1960 and 1980, I grew up in a blizzard of whiteness, surrounded and loved by my maternal German Ukrainian family but without any connection to my paternal Ojibwe family. I had photographs of my father and my Ojibwe kin but no relationship and no idea how to even begin. It wasn't until I was in my midtwenties that I found my father and began taking tentative steps toward the larger Indigenous community, which turned out to have been there all along.

After decades in colonial darkness, I am ready to step into the light.

There is the beat of the drum in that darkened theater and then my voice coming from the back of the stage. I move toward the front, singing each verse louder as the lights come up. When I finish, Karl speaks the words of the Haudenosaunee Thanksgiving Address in Oneida. Then we simply leave the stage. Not explaining the song or our actions or our words is deliberate. We let the audience sit and consider that what feels profoundly alien to them is not alien at all. For one brief moment, they are surrounded by the sounds of this place.

The song that I sing that night had come to me months earlier. I had been driving home from somewhere, running the errands that make up the invisible minutiae of our lives, and listening to news reports about a series of recent suicides in several Anishinaabe communities in northern Ontario. Youths as young as eight and ten years old were taking their own lives. These communities are isolated by design and deliberately underresourced. We describe them as "remote," which begs the question: remote to what? Certainly not remote to places their ancestors lived, where their families still live. But when you strip away everything that makes living somewhere possible, trading promises of a better life for land, you need to deliver on those promises. So as I drove home from those errands, the normality of my life felt obscene against the loss of these children, who would never become ancestors. And the song came out of me like wailing.

I live in the country, rural Niagara. My daily walk goes through a wetland forest, past fields of hay and soybeans. Much of the year, it is a walk noisy with birds and frogs. While I walked my dogs those months before the event, I sang the song again and again so I would remember it. And somehow this song that had been torn out of me while I drove home in the darkness sounded hopeful. It sounded insistent and powerful. I sang it again as I walked, all four verses, the same notes rising and falling in repetition. The verses carry the sounds of loss but also hope. When Karl asked me if I would sing for this event, I knew the song I would sing.

I am Patty, the daughter of Roy, son of Joe and Lula, who are Ojibwe Anishinaabe from Lac Seul, Ontario. When I say that they are from Lac Seul, Ontario, I am referring to the reserve where Joe was registered as an Indian. They are only from that small place because that is where the Indian agent placed their ancestors back in the late nineteenth century, when Canada was creating reserves. Before that, our families would have traveled, understanding themselves to be from a much larger geography.

My father is fond of saying we are descended from Noah and Moses—and indeed, Moses begat Noah, and Noah begat Joe, who married Lula. Lula's mother is Sophie, who apparently saved the life of Isaiah, an Irishman who worked for the Hudson's Bay Company trading goods for furs. Sophie is from Cat Lake, Ontario, and Isaiah's parents, Francis and Sarah, were born in Ireland. It is through my father, Roy, that my roots sink deeply into this place that is called Canada or North America or Turtle Island, twisting through Anishinaabe and possibly Cree ancestors back to the beginning. It is through Roy that my roots entwine with those of the Hudson's Bay Company, which employed Isaiah along with so many other Scots and Irish who found their way into Anishinaabe and Cree lineage. We are Ojibwe Anishinaabe, Caribou Clan, who, along with other subgroups of the larger Hoof Clan, have social responsibilities to the broader community.

I am the daughter of Vicki, who is the daughter of Ann and George. Ann is the daughter of Jacob and Margareta; the granddaughter of Dietrich and Anna, Heinrich and Katharina; the great-granddaughter of Benjamin and Helena, of Heinrich and Maria. My grandmother's family tree is known back to 1772: Germans, moved by Catherine the Great into Russia to displace Ukrainians, who created colonies along the Dnieper River that remained self-contained, and well documented, for two hundred years. In Germany, the Schultzes brewed beer. In the Ukraine, they farmed and then manufactured farm implements. Nothing is known of George's parents except that they were probably Ukrainian farmers. And the man we knew as George was actually my grandmother's second husband, who, like many refugees before and since, found safety in another person's name. It is through my mother, Vicki, that my roots travel through farmland to reach across oceans, searching for a home that is both here and there. It is through Vicki that my roots become interwoven with those of migrants and refugees, rooting us here in shallow but sturdy mats of connection.

I am also the daughter of Jack, my mother's second husband, who adopted me. It is through Jack that my roots run parallel with adoptees—Native children who were scooped by child welfare and placed with white families. For although I was raised by my mother and her second husband, adopted by him and always loved, in other ways I shared the disconnection of other Indigenous children raised by a white adoptive parent.*

Today, I live in wine country, and the geography contains glacial remnants. The soil is variable, with red clay in some places and black earth in others. There are places dense with rocks and minerals, and places where it is less rocky. Wines from the same variety of grape will taste different depending on what the roots sink into—what they wrap around and bring to the surface. Humans are like this too. Knowing what our roots sink into—what they wrap around and bring to the surface—helps us understand the tastes and sensations of our present.

*"When I say that the land is my ancestor, that is a scientific statement"*: Dr. Keolu Fox, a Kānaka Maoli genomic researcher, made this comment at a 2020 presentation. The land itself and the conditions of that land, like altitude and climate, impact our genome just as our human ancestors do. My roots reach out to and draw upon the land of many places, connecting me here, where they reach deeply into the land that created my paternal ancestors.

* The decades between 1960 and 1980 are known colloquially as the time of the Sixties Scoop, when Indigenous children were "scooped" by child welfare workers and placed in white foster homes. The language comes from an interview with a social worker at the time who said that they "just scooped them up." Although I was not taken from my family by child welfare services, my mother's decision to take me south, without maintaining any contact with my Ojibwe family members, had the same social and cultural consequences. I discuss this in more detail in chapter 4.

I tell you who I am so that you will understand the history I am about to share with you. *Becoming Kin* traces the collective history of the United States and Canada, which is also my own history, and yours, but perhaps not one that you are familiar with. My story includes references to Christianity and the Christian scripture and the church, in part because that is the tradition in which I grew up and in part because, whether you are Christian or not, this is also the tradition in which the United States and Canada grew up. The beliefs of those early colonists remain very much a part of our contemporary ideas about how a society ought to function. The Bible is filled with "begats" to remind us that our individual stories are not individual at all.

In this cursory glimpse of my family—which says nothing about my spouse or children, in-laws or outlaws—you can see how my story connects me to places and people. These are relationships I have inherited, relationships with the United States and Canada and the peoples within these borders, relationships with the church, and relationships that stretch across oceans. "History is the story we tell ourselves about how the past explains our present, and the ways we tell it are shaped by contemporary needs," writes poet and activist Aurora Levins Morales, a Jewish Puerto-Rican woman. "All historians have points of view. All of us use some process of selection by which we choose which stories we consider important and interesting . . . storytelling is not neutral."

I will tell you a story, a story of history, in the hopes that it will explain our present and help us weave a new world into being.

Nii'kinaaganaa.

That evening before we go on stage, Karl and I talk about whether Christianity and Indigenous worldviews can ever be reconciled, if there is any common space. He doesn't think so. Karl is Oneida and part of the Haudenosaunee Confederacy. Hundreds of years ago, when it became evident that the newcomers were going to stay, he says, the Confederacy made a treaty with the settlers called the Two Row. This is written in the form of a wampum belt made of oblong purple and white beads, with two purple rows on a white background. The agreement was that we would travel together, the Indigenous peoples and the settlers, each in our own boat but on parallel paths in a relationship guided by peace, honesty, and respect.

The principle of noninterference lives at the root of many Indigenous philosophies and is exemplified in treaties like the Two Row: we would live according to our ways, and the newcomers would live according to theirs. Although colonization is clearly a violation of this treaty, the Haudenosaunee people I know remain committed to it and continue to try to live within these principles.

I agree with Karl's analysis of the newcomers and their religion. As a foreign religion and perpetrator of colonization, Christianity is part of the other boat. He sees Christianity as it exists broadly across the Western world—a faith disconnected from land and strangers, ideas imposed by white Europeans who arrived as guests but almost immediately began to act as autocratic hosts.

But as I understand them, the two rows—those of the Indigenous peoples and the settlers—aren't meant to completely isolate us from each other; they are meant to guide our relationship so that we can live together. And what I know of the worldview of the Anishinaabe is not completely inconsistent with what Christianity could be. I see other possibilities: the original instructions of connection, relationship with land and people. The original instructions as recorded in the Bible are frequently disregarded or redefined in service to settler-colonial ideas about how a society ought to be organized. I think Christianity has the potential to liberate, to actually help us reject those colonial ideas. Throughout the book, I offer Anishinaabe stories and Indigenous knowledge not so that you can claim them as your own but so that they can provide a lens through which you can see your own stories differently. That is part of what I hope to explore in these pages: how we can read these histories differently and find a way to live together in peace, honesty, and respect.

How can we find a way to live in the knowledge that we are all related? How can we become better kin?

All of our creation stories tell of a new people for a new world. But what that new world will look like will depend on what our roots sink into, wrap around, and bring to the surface.

Settlers and newcomers, Black and Indigenous: the history we learn in elementary school is rooted in explorers and settlers. We learn about brave colonists fighting for freedom. We learn about Native people who, despite early Thanksgiving friendship, become dangerous and then mysteriously vanish. The history of slavery is placed comfortably in the past. The American story is one of a war fought to end slavery. The Canadian story about slavery is being the final stop on the Underground Railroad, the place of freedom. We all, settler and newcomer, Black and Indigenous, learn about how these countries were the ones that ended slavery. Somehow in this history, the very people who created the problem are transformed into the ones who saved us.

Together we learn about immigrants and refugees who came here in search of something better and built a great country. The United States and Canada are positioned as communities of safety and refuge for newcomers leaving behind or sublimating their old identities and becoming American or Canadian.

These histories become central truths, and when other histories are told or when somebody makes a racist remark, Americans say with surprise, "That's not who we are!" Your collective memory is filled with stories about cooperation and communities, brave people banding together to defend their home and working together to create something for everyone. Our collective memory is filled with other stories. Other centers.

Sometimes the center is created simply through the act of revolving around it.

What if the things you have been told are *not* who you are? The collective memories of the Black diaspora and Indigenous nations, of Asian laborers and 2SLGBTQIA* people, of Muslims and Jews, and of those who are disabled by a world that is increasingly difficult to navigate are filled with other stories about these same events. Our collective memories contain stories of displacement and disruption, occupation and domination. Even when we try to fit in, when we try to assimilate, we aren't truly accepted.

Activist and academic Angela Davis writes that "our histories never unfold in isolation." These stories—about Western settlement, and Indians who simply vanished, about well-intentioned white folks in the North standing up to slavery—are created and maintained on purpose to protect a particular way of life and a particular social class. Remember: all historians have a point of view, and storytelling is not neutral. These myths are packaged and sold to newcomers and working-class white people so that they will chase promises that

---

* 2SLGBTQIA: Two-spirit, lesbian, gay, bisexual, transgender, queer, intersex, asexual. Most Indigenous societies did not recognize a strict gender binary, being perhaps more comfortable with transitional spaces than European Christians. Binaries create exceptions, and exceptions require names and ever-expanding rainbows and letters to make sure everyone is included.

were never meant for them. The stories are like isolated snapshots of the American dream, with important context cropped out of the image. Isolated stories are told in part so that the whole picture cannot be seen. The creation story we have been taught is incomplete. It is incomplete, but it is not inaccessible, and nothing stays buried forever. These histories are emerging, and the stories are being told. What would happen if you listened? What would happen if you, the churches and countries who settled upon us, listened to our histories and heard the good news that we have for you?

Biskaabiiyang: returning to ourselves.

Colonization has gotten inside our heads. It is more than driving cars and talking on iPhones, more than the food we eat or where we shop. It is how we think. We often put colonialism in the past, dressing it up in sixteenth-century costumes. But as Patrick Wolfe has said, colonialism is a process and not an event. Settler colonialism came to stay in the Americas in the sixteenth century, but it neither started there, nor has it stopped. It cut its teeth on the Crusades, where the rape and violence enacted on Jews and Muslims were the price of Christian freedom. A violence that persists and finds expression in the burnings of mosques and synagogues, shootings, and travel bans. It sharpened its blade on the repeated expulsions of Jewish people from Europe and the reconquest of the Iberian Peninsula, which banished Muslims from Spain. It consolidated its power over women through the fires of the witch burnings. And it arrived on these shores with the authority of the Doctrine of Discovery tucked beneath its arm, settling into our lands and our heads, shaping everything about how we live. It is an ongoing process of destruction and replacement, destroying Indigenous beliefs and lifeways and replacing them with churches and board meetings.

Wendy Makoons Geniusz and Leanne Betasamosake Simpson both write about biskaabiiyang as returning to our own Anishinaabe way of thinking. When we return to ourselves, we undo the colonialism that has gotten inside our heads.

We can only do this if we are willing to understand our history differently, if we take our stories out of isolation and put them together. We need to revisit the stories we tell ourselves—about how we got here—and see something different, see something that allows us to become relatives again. To put back together what modern ideas about race have torn apart. "Ultimately what we inherit are relationships and our beliefs about them," writes Aurora Levins Morales. "We can't alter the actions of our ancestors, but we can decide what to do with the social relations they left us." In order to understand these relationships, we need to listen to the histories that we were *not* told so that we can begin to remember the things buried beneath the histories we *were*.

In her book *Knowing Otherwise*, Alexis Shotwell describes various forms of knowledge. She notes that as individuals and as communities, we hold knowledge in ways that we can articulate or explain to others and also in ways that are less tangible—knowledge that we can't articulate in the same way. Some things we can identify or describe, and then some things we just *know*. Sometimes we don't have the language for what we're trying to explain, or it doesn't even occur to us that it needs explaining. We just *know*. This unspoken knowledge binds us together, with common courtesy and common sense that are really only common to our particular group. These are things like body memory, such as the way that your hands know how to do things without you thinking through each step. It's also emotional knowledge: the way that certain things make you feel but for which you lack language. There are also unspoken truths: assumptions about how the world works that we all accept.

The trick is to get those assumptions from where they rest inside you or inside our broader society out to a place where you can articulate them. To move those unspoken things from implicit to explicit so they can be challenged or reconsidered.

Historian Roxanne Dunbar-Ortiz talks about the process of "unforgetting." The divisions between us are only possible because we have forgotten our history, forgotten our creation stories. Forgotten how to articulate the knowledge that is held in unspoken ways. Unforgetting is the process of reclaiming that knowledge—of moving these truths that our society holds silently out to where we can articulate them and examine them. Then we can see if they really are a center worth revolving around, worth the emotional response they engender.

This is a book about Indigenous reality and experience, but I will speak often about Black experience and reality as well—not because it is mine but because it is connected. That connection is one of the things I am working to unforget. In *Beloved*, the masterpiece by Toni Morrison, she describes Paul D's escape from a chain gang, and in that escape, she writes about the Cherokee. In that passage, Morrison remembers the removals and the sickness. She remembers relationship. And I think often about something that Dr. Tiya Miles said about history in a discussion that I once organized. Miles, an African American historian, said there are gaps in our stories: gaps in Black studies where Native people should be and gaps in Native studies where Black people should be. We are not discrete categories of people upon which colonialism acts in different ways; we are a Venn diagram with areas of huge overlap. The gaps Miles refers to are the work of settler colonialism pulling us apart. And so I situate this book in that area of overlap, in that area of relationship rather than in the edges. That is the center I will revolve around and create.

This book, in helping us reclaim our interconnected histories, will take us to a place of becoming good relatives. We are all related, and we will see in the next chapter that all creation stories tell us this. But what does it mean to be *good* relatives—to not only recognize our kinship but to be *good* kin? Because, for Indigenous peoples, kinship is not simply a matter of being like a brother or sister to somebody. It carries specific responsibilities depending on the kind of relationship we agree upon. An aunt has different responsibilities than a brother. If we are going to be kin, then we must accept that these relationships come with responsibility. In our settler-colonial context, relationships between us are built on a paternalistic foundation: charity and good works, helping the less fortunate. Those who are part of the society that created the problem become the ones who think they can solve it. So we must move from recognizing the *fact* of our relationship to actually existing together in *reciprocal* relationships.

How do we restore relationships and balance to what has been made so precarious? The promises of the white Christian West have failed to materialize, and we are, socially and literally, on a precipice. How do we go from living in isolated silos to becoming good relatives? How does the church stop running wild and unshod and put down roots that reach deeply into the ground? We can draw on everything that our roots have pushed through and around and pulled forward. Rather than cutting off our roots because we are ashamed or afraid of what we will find, we can learn our history. We can reimagine the relationships we have inherited, and we can take up our responsibilities to each other.

At some point in the distant past, we began to pick things up and take them with us.

At some point, archaic humans not only fashioned tools; they began to carry these tools with them from one place to another. They began to carry decorative objects and things that held memory of other places and people. They decorated themselves with memory and story. They carried fire and the tools with which they created fire. And around these fires, our long-dead ancestors began to gather together, holding these objects and sharing the stories that were already ancient. Stories tied to feather and stone, tools and ceremonial items that explained who they were and how they were connected to the world around them. They began to carry bundles.

My bundle is a tangible thing. It is a box topped with a blanket that contains stones and pipes, an eagle feather, and a brass cup. It contains the fundamental medicines of the Ojibwe: tobacco and sage, sweetgrass and cedar. It contains matches and a lighter and a small cast-iron pan. These things hold story and memory, responsibility and care. They remind me of people and places, ceremonies and obligations I am only beginning to understand. My bundle is a container that holds knowledge and the responsibilities that I carry with me.

You have a bundle too. Think of what you would gather if you had to flee, the objects that mean the most to you. They aren't just things; you know that. You look at them and see memory and history, connection and relationship. The items in our bundles have ancestors too: they have stories to tell us about the lives they led before they arrived in our hands. These things that are precious to us connect us to relatives and histories, to memories and stories unspoken and relatives we may or may not wish to claim.

When I say return to yourself and pick up your bundle, I am asking you to look at those things with new eyes. Listen to their full history and remember your relationships and obligations.

Biskaabiiyang.

Just as I did that evening years ago with Karl, we are, all of us, together standing in the dark, waiting to hear the heartbeat of a new beginning. Waiting to find our voice and become the people who our ancestors promised we could become.

We've been here before. History is not a clean story of progress, no straight trajectory from barbarism to civilization, ever marching forward. We live in a constant state of tension between equity and inequity, with people or societies holding more or less power in different places and times.

We need to go back to the beginning—or, rather, to a story of new beginnings—in order to start again.

Most cultures have a flood story. Just as a creation story tells us how we began, a flood story can tell us how to rebuild. In the Anishinaabe story, which we will visit in some detail later, Nanaboozhoo, a central figure in Anishinaabe stories, together with the animals rebuilt Turtle Island with a handful of mud gathered from deep below the floodwaters.

In order to return to our original instructions—in order to unforget and pick up that handful of mud—we, too, must travel through the floodwaters. The first part of this book is that journey. We are living during a time of cataclysm and upheaval. We are in a flood event, and we have the potential to create something new. But first we need to swim deep down through the waters of history, and that is hard. The second part of the book, then, is about rebuilding. In the second part, we take our handful of mud and begin to rebuild our relationships with land and with each other and then mobilize those relationships to create something new.

Each chapter ends with a section called "Aambe." *Aambe* is an Anishinaabe word that can mean "Attention!" or "Come on, let's go!" On this journey together, instead of going straight to the point, we will look at what is in the floodwaters and mud of history. We will see what the flotsam and jetsam can teach us. And at the end of each chapter, there will be something you can do, something tangible to move you forward on this journey we take together.

※　※　※

The Anishinaabe tradition includes a series of prophecies, eight in total, that are identified as a series of fires. *Prophecy* is a fraught term as we often think of it like a psychic foretelling of the future. But it is more of a proclamation: a statement of truth that takes on meaning in particular circumstances. Fires are places of community, where we come together against a gathering dark. But for the Anishinaabe, fire is more than that. Dr. Paulette Steeves talks about *pyro-epistemology*, a term she coined in 2012 to describe the fire-based system of knowledge of the Anishinaabeg. For the Anishinaabe, fire is an environmental technology used to shape the landscape, to cleanse and make space for new growth. In that context, these fires are more than gathering places. They are wildfires—episodes of social and spiritual cleansing, of making room for new beginnings.

One of these fires, or prophecies, speaks of a people who would come from across the water. These people might come with the face of kinship or the face of death. If they come with the face of kinship, the new knowledge that they bring could be joined with ours. But the warnings by which we would know which face they would wear are stark. The prophecy warns of weapons and greed, of poisoned water with fish you can't eat.

The Seventh Fire talks about a new people emerging: people who would retrace their steps and pick up the bundles that were lost. You may have the objects, but you have forgotten what they mean, or perhaps new histories have been written on top of old ones. Picking up your bundle means looking at these things differently. This prophecy talks about a choice that the light-skinned people would need to make between two roads. One road is lush and green, and the other is black and charred, and walking on it will cut their feet. If the light-skinned race chooses well, the Eighth fire will be lit: a fire of peace, love, and community.

Biskaabiiyang.

I can't help but think about the choices our colonial governments make that have left the land black and charred, choices that cut. I think about the Alberta oil sands and tailing ponds leaking into the waterways. I think about Water Protectors at Standing Rock being hit by water cannons in subzero weather. I wrote much of this book during the pandemic, as political leaders weighed the economy against our lives, and I think of how they tried to decide how many deaths are acceptable to rescue capitalism.

And I also think of the lush, green road: about community gardens and farming collectives and kinship. I think about all the conversations that my friend Kerry and I have had on our podcast with people who are choosing to build community instead of wealth and transforming the places where they live. I think about the weeds that grow along the side of highways and how my son looks at them and sees a green path that ensures the survival of insects. The green path is there. We just need to shift our perspective.

Nii'kinaaganaa.

## Aambe

As we prepare to reconsider the history that we have learned, look for Black and Indigenous people. Look for us in your life, on your bookshelf, in the music you listen to and the movies or television you watch. Look for us on your social media feed. Look for us in the collective nostalgia of your country. Don't try to read too much into our presence or absence. Just notice.

Where are we?

# CHAPTER 1

# CREATION: HOW WE GOT HERE

Sometimes the center is created by the act of revolving around it. Creation stories are that kind of center. We circle around them, coming back to these fundamental narratives again and again, looking for clues about our relationship with the world around us, for clues about how we got here and why we are here.

The Anishinaabe creation story, like that of the Christian narrative, begins with a thought. From this thought comes a breath, and with that breath all things come into existence, like seeds flying into the universe: stars and planets, earth, land, and water, plants, animals, and finally humans. Earth is understood to be a woman, our Mother, who preceded man. From her come all living things, and water is her blood. After all things were made, the Creator takes four parts of Mother Earth and blows into them, and with this breath man is created. Humans are the *last* form of life to be created, lowered down onto the earth, the least and neediest of all creation. This is a lesson in humility: We are the least of all creation. Creation existed without us, and despite everything we have done to her, she continues to provide for us.

"When all of these beings were created, they promised Gichi-manidoo that they would live together and help all other levels of Creation survive." This is an important teaching that Wendy

Makoons Geniusz draws on in her book *Our Knowledge Is Not Primitive*. Not only did each successive level of creation need what had come before, but they collectively promised to care for each other. She notes that of all the layers of creation, only the rocks, natural forces, and spirits would survive independently. But they would not be content if they survived alone because they could not keep their promise to ensure survival for all others.

Nii'kinaaganaa.

The Creator provided all beings, human and not human, with original instructions: information about our responsibilities and obligations. Many traditions have this idea of original instructions. The early commands to Adam and Eve, the words of Moses—these could be seen as original instructions. The words of Jesus form the original instructions to the church. Part of our responsibility as human beings is to remember these and then build our lives around them. To remember ourselves.

Unlike the Christian creation story, the Anishinaabe creation story does not contain a fall or an expulsion. Our expulsion only happens later: at the time of colonization, when the Western world arrives at our doorstep. In our story, Nanaboozhoo, one of the original humans, walks the world meeting and naming the animals. He meets other people and lives in relationship with them. Like in the story of Cain exiled to the land of Nod, there is no explanation for who these other people are; they just are.

The Anishinaabe also have a story of wandering, a circling of sorts, around the lands in which the Creator placed us. We begin in the West and move east through lands of water and wild rice, and then centuries later we circle back, leaving communities dotting the lands and waters above and below the Great Lakes. Our migration was not a search for home; it was a return.

The history of the Christian West revolves around a different center. Beginning with possibility, it ends in punishment as the first man and woman are cast from Eden. It reads itself into the captivity of the Hebrews in Egypt and their conquest of Canaan, a pattern of expulsion and conquest that would repeat when the church fled Jerusalem and became Rome and then left Europe and subjugated the Americas and the Pacific. It is a story of continual wandering and searching for a place to make a home, often through violence. This is a central theme in literature and movies; from *Wagon Train* to *Star Trek*, Americans admire this desire to boldly go and then bravely defend themselves from those who resent discovery. Discovery, after all, has never been good for those it has uncovered. It inevitably leads to exploitation and death.

Christians are unmoored, landless people. Maybe that disconnection from land is what has led to other disconnections. Steve Heinrichs, an activist and writer who calls himself a settler Christian, spoke in an interview about this and his attempt to reconnect: "I don't simply ask, God what are you trying to say to me through the land? I do something which seems very foreign to me—is coming from Indigenous teachers who are telling me, 'Ask the water! Ask the river, what's it saying?' And so, I'm just trying to be quiet and listen." I remember learning in church that this world was not our home, that we were strangers in a strange land and that our hope was in heaven. That changes how you look at things. Instead of listening to what the land might have to say for itself, you listen only for what God might be saying through it, reducing it to an empty vessel. It diminishes our investment in the world around us and disconnects us from everything, including people, because we don't listen to them either. Relationships become a means to an end, a way to evangelize people so they, too, can become unmoored and disconnected from everything except Jesus.

❋  ❋  ❋

There is another creation story, the one that scientists tell using mitochondria. Mitochondria are tiny powerhouses in our cells that generally carry DNA from mother to child. By tracing mitochondrial DNA, scientists follow maternal lines back in time. They follow breadcrumbs across the globe to identify relationships and uncover migration patterns.

Calling this woman Mitochondrial *Eve* is a bit strange because if she existed, it was in what is now eastern or maybe southern Africa, not the Tigris-Euphrates River valley. She probably ate dates, not apples, and lived with others like her, not with a man in a garden. Her existence, this ancient mother whose story we read in the fragments of our own DNA, is written over and replaced with a Christian narrative.

Talking about ancient ancestors as African is risky. This claim carries modern assumptions about what it means to be African into a history that did not exist in that way. When we talk about humanity beginning in Africa, it sounds like those evolutionary charts you still see in museums: humanity began in Africa (hunched over and Black) and then progressed to European (standing tall and white). Modern evolution is still the story of colonists, missionaries, and industry bringing civilization to Stone Age people. The history of Europe and now America is told as one of linear progress rather than a story of change. It's as if these people, like uncontacted Amazonian tribes or the Indigenous peoples of the Andaman Islands, exist outside of our timeline and need to be modernized, rescued.

We also now know that what we've believed about our common human ancestry is troubled by other children of this ancient mother—so-called archaic humans, who include the long-past

Neanderthals and Denisovans. These are people who no longer exist but whose DNA we carry within us. An insistence on fitting humanity into a single creation story becomes complicated and has consequences for those who don't share that story.

Ideas about ancient roots, as if there existed some pure lineage from which the rest of us have branched off into lesser beings, are used by some to establish legitimacy over others they see as newcomers or offshoots of the truth, something that Ben Kiernan discusses in his book *Blood and Soil*. The modern church and the modern US state imagine a straight line connecting them through the Reformation to Rome and, for some, all the way to the garden of Eden. Everyone else needs to be corrected or pruned off. In this chapter, we will see how the church and the United States that it helped to found used that connection to justify their authority over those they believed were wrong and those they "discovered."

Creation stories speak of emergence. The Genesis creation story places the emergence of people in Mesopotamia, the region of the Tigris and Euphrates, where grain and large cities like Uruk developed. The Anishinaabe creation story places us in the woodlands north of what is now called Lake Superior. The Hopi, in a land of deep canyons, emerged from a hole in the ground. The Inuit emerged from holes in the ice. Our creation stories situate us in a particular place, with particular relationships.

Creation stories, whether Christian or Hebrew, Anishinaabe or Hopi, aren't meant to be histories—not in the sense that the Western world has invented the idea of history as an unbiased set of facts. They are meant to explain who we are and create a communal sense of self.

The Anishinaabe word for *north* holds our history: giiwedin, the north, contains the idea of going home. The stem or root word *giiwe* means to "go home," and it refers not to the earliest people who filled this place or even to others who left. There is a similar word in Cree, and the oral traditions of the Anishinaabe and the Cree tell us that it refers to the great ice sheets that came south and then returned north—or home—leaving the landscape permanently changed. The word for "wind" is *noodin*, so giiwedin, which contains a stem from that word, *–din*, can also be understood as *north wind*. Our language, Anishinaabemowin, contains history that includes memories of glaciers arriving and then retreating.

What fascinated me about this when I heard Josh Manitowabi speak about it a few years ago was not simply the etymology. All words contain history and fragments of the deep past that may or may not be present in the contemporary meaning. What fascinated me was that the language speakers *knew* this etymology. More than simply including the root words *go home* and *wind*, the oral history of the Nehiyaw (Cree) and Anishinaabeg included the knowledge of *what* was going home. We knew about the great sheets of ice long before Enlightenment-era scientists figured it out by studying the erratic dispersal of boulders in the Alps.

The last glacial period, extending from about 115,000 to 11,700 years ago, covered the top half of what is now North America, with maximum coverage occurring about twenty-two thousand years ago. This means that our oral history goes back tens of thousands of years. It goes back far enough that our word for *north* not only knows about glaciers; it knows they had not always been there.

❋　❋　❋

Across the Americas are many nations whose creation stories and belief systems are sometimes very different. Just as the garden of

Eden is located geographically by the Tigris and Euphrates Rivers, our creation stories are also located geographically in places all over the continents. We were used to multiple creation stories, peoples whose circling created their own centers. We understood how to live together with these multiple eddies, circular currents that draw up nutrients from the colder, deeper waters.

This was not true in Europe. At the time that Columbus set sail, Europe was primarily Christian. Ancient Rome had reached to the edges of Europe, and then Western Christianity followed Roman roads, writing its own story on top of earlier stories, and for a thousand years the people of this small peninsula of Asia had the same creation story. When these European Christians arrived in worlds they called new, they were again confronted with new stories, with unfamiliar people, and they had to figure out where *we* fit in. Who were we? If the Bible talked about *everything*, as they thought that it did, then surely it must mention us somewhere.

Over and over, these settlers have written themselves on top of our stories, taking small parts of our stories and fitting them into the biblical narrative. Even when they did listen to our stories, it was only to hear fragments of their own story, not to understand ours. They had good news for *us*, after all; why would they think we might have good news for *them*? Just as humanity's ancient mother was transformed into Mitochondrial Eve, we, too, have been recast into the Bible's story.

Some believe that we are the descendants of Noah's son Shem, from whom also came Arabs and Israelites. Others believed that we are Israel's lost tribes, the ten who went into exile and never returned. The idea of people mysteriously vanishing has romantic appeal, whether we are talking about lost tribes of Israel or the Anasazi who lived in what is now the southwestern United States. When people vanish, you can write your own history on top of theirs, replacing them with a story you like better.

Archeology also writes its stories on top of ours. As recently as 1912, the head curator of the Smithsonian Institute was arguing that "Indians" had only been here for three thousand years, and for decades he resisted evidence of an earlier presence. In 1908, George McJunkin, a ranch foreman and former enslaved person, discovered the bones of long-extinct bison and stone tools in Folsom, New Mexico. This find pushed scientists' understanding of human presence earlier, to ten thousand years before the present. Throughout the twentieth century, additional finds like the Clovis culture—a paleolithic culture identified by a particular style of flaking to create stone tools—would place scattered human presence in North America about eleven thousand to thirteen thousand years ago, just as the Ice Age was ending.

Giiwedin.

Our oral histories contain other clues to human presence in what would become the Americas during the Pleistocene, that geological epoch that lasted more than two million years and ended when the great sheets of ice finally retreated north. Dr. Paulette Steeves is a Cree-Métis paleontologist whose research begins by listening to the oral histories of the people whose land is being excavated and studied. In her book *The Indigenous Paleolithic of the Western Hemisphere*, Steeves writes about the teratornis, a giant bird with wingspans ranging from twelve to eighteen feet in what is now North America and up to twenty-three feet in what is now South America. Oral histories across the hemisphere talk about thunderbirds: great birds that kidnapped children and fought serpents. Other oral histories talk about large mammals and celestial events that connect in multiple ways with geological, paleontological, and archeological records. Based on her research, Steeves argues for Indigenous presence in North America more than 130,000 years ago, noting that there is no *good* reason to insist otherwise. Evidence, she points out, is often not found because it is not looked for.

Steeves also argues against the existence of a Clovis *culture*, which flattens an entire hemisphere of cultures into a monolith based on a single artifact and remains the standard timeframe against which all other finds are measured. This is, she argues, rather like identifying global car users as a single culture. But that is how Indigenous cultures of the Western Hemisphere are often seen: as a monolith. We are seen as a single culture, a single people who haven't been here that long anyway.

Giiwedin.

The idea that eventually became the Bering Strait theory was first proposed by a Spanish missionary in 1590 to explain how we got here. He speculated that there must be land connecting this new world with Asia and that people had walked across it. A land mass did exist between Asia and North America in the Far North: the now-submerged continent called Berengia. During the Ice Age, the glaciers held so much water that people could live in areas that are now below sea level. There is a field of underwater archeology that excavates these submerged histories.

It is possible that ancient relatives crossed this land mass, possibly hunting mammoth herds and possibly following these herds down a corridor between two glaciers into what would become North America. But there are problems with relying solely on Berengia to explain the presence of people on this continent. There are discoveries of human presence in *South* America between thirty-five thousand and forty thousand years ago, much earlier than this theory suggests. And human footprints recently found in the White Sands

National Park in New Mexico are at least twenty-one thousand years old—ten thousand years earlier than Clovis.

Steeves notes that we accept that about sixty thousand years ago humans crossed an ocean to get to Australia, but we deny the same possibilities for ancient travel to those indigenous to the Americas. We must have walked, bedraggled and forlorn, wandering into the landscape by accident. If animals like camels, which emerged in what is now the Americas, could travel between hemispheres, then why couldn't humans? New theories continue to challenge old ones, and by the time these words are published, there might already be new archeological information or new ways of reading old information.

Giiwedin.

Indigenous peoples have creation stories that root us in our own places, that tell us who we are and what our relationship is with our Creator and the world around us. Forcing us into a different creation story begins our disconnection from the land. *We have always been here*: this is how we understand ourselves. And it is true, even if we did migrate from somewhere else more than one hundred thousand years ago. Our own creation stories are filled with migration and travel. But this land is where we emerged as peoples; this is where we developed our political systems and cosmologies. This is where we fell to earth or emerged from the ground or otherwise formed our identities as distinct peoples.

Our words and our stories hold this knowledge. Our origin story is valuable because it not only tells us who we are; it tells us who we can become.

※　※　※

For many people, history begins in Mesopotamia, with the cultivation of wheat, and the subsequent development of cities, and the expansion of more complex societies that created government and knowledge. Europeans, and then Americans, saw themselves as heirs of ancient Rome, replicating their architecture and plantation-style agricultural systems.

Known as the Neolithic Revolution, the domestication of grain and the invention of farming created a sharp line dividing history into before and after. It took place about eleven thousand years ago. By even the most conservative estimates of human presence in the Americas, we were already here. We may have been here for thousands of years when the cities of Ur began to store grain. The colonists did not bring a Neolithic Revolution of farming and agriculture to us; we had our own.

In his book *1491*, Charles C. Mann outlines at least three Neolithic Revolutions in the Americas. In what is now South America, tribes domesticated potatoes and manioc. In what is now the eastern United States, other tribes developed sunflower, sumpweed, and goosefoot. Maize, or corn, emerged in what is now Mexico. Although each of these three—potatoes and manioc; sunflower, sumpweed, and goosefoot; and maize—transformed the societies that developed them, it is maize that transformed the hemisphere. Through centuries of people hybridizing it and selecting for traits, a grass called teosinte became maize. It traveled to Peru, where it was slightly changed, and then back to Mexico, where it transformed the civilization there. Then it traveled across the continent, becoming dozens of varieties, and eventually arrived in the East. Maize is so central to so many civilizations, from the Mayans in the West to the Haudenosaunee in the East, that it features in their creation stories, connecting the arrival of corn with their emergence as a people.

*We are maize.* The original peoples of the Americas emerged as nations after centuries of merging and splitting, and although we are all related, we retain characteristics related to the land where we emerged. We continue to develop, and as a result of colonization, many of us live in new urban centers, forming communities without our communities. We are changing, and something new is emerging.

Just as corn is central to the Indigenous peoples whose land is suited for agriculture, wild rice, or manomin, is central to those whose land is filled with lakes connected to running water. The vast woodlands north of Lake Superior were known to the Anishinaabe as Manitou gitigenan, or the "Great Mystery's Garden." In Mesopotamia, life began in a garden where the Tigris and Euphrates Rivers meet, and the Neolithic Revolution centered around wheat. For the Anishinaabe, life began in Manitou gitigenan.

Wild rice has been a challenge for western agriculture to domesticate. It isn't really rice but a grainlike grass, and it grows in the shallow waters of lakes. Unlike corn, it wasn't developed through a hybridization process; we eat it much as it was planted by the Creator. Anishinaabe communities, across the vast geography of our territories, dot the lakes where it is found. Just as in hunting season, when we went to where the animals were, in ricing season, we settled near the rice beds. Many of our contemporary reservations are near former rice beds.

*We are manomin.* The original peoples exist across the Americas in the distinct ways that we were created, fallen to earth or rising from holes as beings in this new world. We are in relationship with our Creator and the other beings created with us, as essential to the existence of the land and water on which we live as the land and water are essential to our existence. This is where we live and die, our bodies returning to earth, where they are taken up by plants and animals only to return to earth again. Webs of reciprocal, cyclical relationships.

Multiple creation stories, emerging from multiple gardens, describe the relationships of multiple peoples. There is not a single story to which we must all be reconciled. Not a single story with a single message. Not a single narrative that provides its bearer with authority and power to control the lives of others.

Western thinkers—whether theologians, historians, or scientists—look for how we arrived here so that they can position us as simply *earlier* settlers. This perspective of us—as people who wandered off from the garden, who wandered off from the truth—became a basis for authority over us. In trying to fit the new world into the Christian story, the Jesuit theologian José de Acosta, an influential sixteenth-century priest whose writing laid the foundation for many of the beliefs that shaped the Christian West, began to disconnect us from the land. Acosta organized Christian beliefs so that they justified the enslavement of indigenes and Africans, justified what would become a racial hierarchy of intelligence and moral capability, and justified colonialism and the white Christian hegemony that followed. It was Acosta who redefined Christian suffering to mean living alongside unbelievers—something we hear echoes of today in the way that many Christians feel persecuted by the war on Christmas or taking official prayer out of school. Acosta developed the imperial theology that underpins how "Christian" countries have behaved and continue to behave.

Having a single creation story not only made ours wrong; it created a power differential that placed European Christians, who knew the truth, above the Indigenous peoples, who lived in darkness. Europe, dominated as it was by Christians, had a single creation story and had previously dealt with difference by eliminating or absorbing it. But the Americas had many; we had learned to live with multiplicity.

European settlers in this "new world" saw themselves in the Israelite conquest of Canaan, when the Hebrew people crossed the Jordan River to invade and possess the land. The settlers were reading themselves into the text in a way that appropriates the narrative and promise that was meant for the Jewish people. There are Gentiles throughout the text: Hagar, Rahab, and Ruth; Jethro, Luke, and Cornelius. The cities of Nineveh and Babylon. Nahum, the Canaanite woman who argues with Jesus, Philemon, and so many others. Some of these people entered the story of Israel as good relatives, forming reciprocal relationships that contributed to the building of a people who were to be a blessing to all. Others entered through conquest and dominion, imposing relations of power and control. Their actions and their ends should have served as a cautionary tale rather than a model to follow.

What if the early European colonists, instead of thinking of us as having wandered from the truth, had considered our own emergence as people in relationship with this place? What if they had seen God's presence in this place instead of emptiness and absence? What if the settlers, instead of reenacting the conquest of Canaan, had pursued relationship? What if they had sought kinship?

Nii'kinaaganaa.

## Aambe

Land acknowledgments are statements recognizing the Indigenous people who lived in the area, as well as those who still live here and who contribute to the existence of this place. At its worst, the impulse to use land acknowledgments is akin to thinking that admitting that you stole a TV set means it's okay to keep it. Such statements at the beginning of an event—"This is the traditional land of the Anishinaabe and Haudenosaunee people"—can be empty and performative.

At best, land acknowledgments recognize relationships, the price that Indigenous people have paid for the existence of this place, and reflect on tangible things people can do. Southridge Community Church in St. Catharines, Ontario, is starting to use land acknowledgments in its church services, reflecting on what it means to talk about grace and blessings on land that was stolen and in a place where the blessings that their church community experiences come at a price. This practice has led members to connect with local organizers to learn how they can work for justice alongside Indigenous peoples without only seeing them as potential converts.

Land acknowledgments are a moment to pause and reflect on the relationship that exists between the current residents and those who were displaced. What does it mean to live on stolen land? You may not be guilty of the act of dispossession, but it is a relationship that you have inherited.

Who lived in your area before colonization? Who still lives there?

# CHAPTER 2

# COLONIZATION: THE HUNGER OF BIG BROTHER

The wendigo, an Anishinaabe creature, is a man who became a monster. The original wendigo, according to Anishinaabe storyteller and historian Basil Johnston, was a man who lived with his family beside a lake, and life was good. He and his family had enough to eat and enough to live on, and they were satisfied.

But things changed, as they do, and life became harder. There were fewer animals, and fish were harder to catch. The man and his family began to starve. The man prayed, and nothing changed. He eventually sought help from a sorcerer, who gave him a potion that he was to drink in the morning.

It worked—unfortunately. After taking the potion, the wendigo went to a village and, unaware of his own transformation, looked at the people and saw beavers. The man killed and ate them—the entire village. He didn't bring any food home to his family, and he didn't stop to think about what he was eating, about these beavers who had been people. He grew larger and hungrier. His insatiable hunger would drive him to chew off his own lips and eat them if there was nothing else to eat.

The wendigo is a creature of winter, and during his transformation, chunks of ice formed within him, the bleakness of the winter season becoming an inextricable part of him. He is often understood as a cautionary tale against greed and consumption, but he emerged out of need and desperation. The man and his family were starving.

In the fall of 1907, Jack Fiddler, the leader of an Ojibwe clan in northern Ontario, was charged with murder. He and his brother, Joseph, were accused of killing Wahsakapeequay, a woman who they and others believed had been possessed by a wendigo. This possession posed a threat to the community as the people were already starving and in precarious circumstances. The wendigo spirit would provoke violence and cannibalism, so when attempts to drive out the spirit failed, they killed her. The federal police in Canada arrested the Fiddler brothers and held them for trial and execution, thus doing to the brothers what the state was accusing them of doing to the woman Wahsakapeequay.

I don't know if the wendigo is a real spirit or a cautionary tale. But I know that some hungers pose a threat to our communities. And I know that when we move to protect ourselves, the state acts quickly to assert its power over us.

In her book *All Our Relations*, Tanya Talaga relates a similar story that was told to her by Cree writer and chief Edmund Metatawabin. Big Brother is always hungry, Edmund told her; he is a voracious monster that never stops eating. He is so hungry that he turns his little brother into a slave and forces him to go out looking for food.

But no matter what Little Brother brings—trees for lumber, diamonds from the earth, fish from the rivers—it is never enough. Edmund asked, "When will Little Brother finally stand up and say enough?"

❈  ❈  ❈

Hungers were rising on the European peninsula of Asia. Powerful men and women grasped for more power, enclosing their lands and forcing peasants off their farms and into cities. After centuries of traveling to India and China by land, they looked to the sea for a way around the Muslim Caliphates with whom they were frequently at war. Columbus and others set sail for India and arrived in islands they called the West Indies. The emerging middle class meant emerging power for men who also grasped for more power, and the burning years began.

The witch hunts were part of this grasping for power and not the work of ignorant people. For hundreds of years, the church had given little care or thought to the small magics of daily life. Women did much of the medical care, as well as assisting with childbirth. They sold goods at market and brewed beer. Although feudal life was far from ideal, it existed largely outside of waged labor. This meant that the contributions of men and women were seen as complementary rather than competitive: men and women both supported the family and the community without one being seen as more important or one's labor being valued as more legitimate. Silvia Federici, in her book *Caliban and the Witch*, connects the emergence of capitalism with the ideology of the witch hunts and describes them as a strategy to control and, if necessary, eliminate women. Witch hunts literally terrorized women into submission, removed them from the social sphere, and resulted in thousands of deaths across Europe and then the colonies. Over time, these ideas about inherent evil and dangerous powers were transferred from women to Black and Indigenous peoples, terrorizing us into submission, removing us from the social sphere, and resulting in thousands of deaths.

"Settler colonialism destroys in order to replace," writes Patrick Wolfe, an academic who studied global settler colonialism. His work describes both the ethnic cleansing that began the moment that Columbus arrived, as well as the replacement of our beliefs and relationships. From the very beginning, the newcomers worked to destroy Indigenous people. Their aim included destroying our beliefs about ourselves and our relationship with the seen and unseen world and replacing them with European Christian beliefs. We were made to fit into their history, their cosmology, and their economic system.

When we talk about demonizing or dehumanizing people as part of that destroy-and-replace process, we can take another important lesson from the wendigo. Although he sees beavers instead of people—as something he could consume rather than as humans, like him—*the people* are unchanged. They may appear to be beavers to the wendigo, but in the stories they remain human. It is the man who consumes them who is transformed. It is the man who consumes them who is dehumanized.

Columbus never actually landed in what would become the United States, and yet he has been successfully remade into the first immigrant, the first American. This Americanizing of Columbus took place after US independence and represented a break with Britain, a reimagining of the roots of this new country. Historian Roxanne Dunbar-Ortiz points out that this Americanizing of an Italian man took place at a time when Italian immigrants faced significant racism and exclusion. He may have been Italian, but he wasn't like them. He was American.

Columbus and the Spanish led the Catholic colonization of the Caribbean and what we now know as the Central and Southern

Americas. Spain's reach would extend through what is now Florida and across the continent to Nevada and California before being pushed back to the current Mexico-US border in the nineteenth century. The Aztec empire had a political system that was so familiar to the Spaniards that, after conquest, the Spanish simply stepped in and took the tribute, a kind of tax that smaller city-states had paid to the Aztec empire, for themselves. But where the Aztecs generally left the smaller cities to function independently as long as they paid their tribute, the Spaniards imposed and expanded systems of agriculture and mining that enriched the upper classes and enslaved the Indigenous populations.

On the Atlantic coast, it was the English and Dutch who arrived and set down largely Protestant colonies, while French Catholics settled along the northern Atlantic and St. Lawrence Seaway. Together, they carved up a continent that already had nations and peoples living on it. Although the early colonists remarked on gardens and well-kept forests, they also maintained that the Natives weren't really using the land—or at least we weren't using it "properly."

Developers still say that it "isn't being used" when they want to develop an area of land. But that only means that people aren't using it in a particular way. Plants and animals are using it. People are using it. It is never a matter of *whether* the land is being used. It is *how* and *who* that matter—that prioritize one set of uses over all others and give one group the right to push aside another.

It is part of American mythology that Indigenous peoples did not have a concept of land ownership and that Europeans did, which is how the Dutch were able to "buy" Manhattan for a handful of beads and trinkets. According to this mythology, the takeover of land from Indigenous people wasn't so much a swindle as a misunderstanding.

Land ownership is a strange thing, and Europeans themselves were just beginning to develop ideas about land as a commodity in the fifteenth and sixteenth centuries. Only in the seventeenth and eighteenth centuries would land become fully disconnected from the people who lived on it—something you could speculate in for profit. At the time of early European settlement, land ownership was understood differently. You owned land because you used it, not because you bought it. And just as the colonists believed their rights derived from a superior lineage that connected European empires to the Roman conquest of Europe, seeing themselves in the way that they read the Hebrew conquest of Canaan, their entitlement to land relied on their beliefs about the how and who of land use. They were, after all, using it correctly.

We don't own land the way that we own a car or a book. If I want to move to another city, I can't just pick up my land and take it somewhere else. I don't own the mineral rights beneath the surface, nor do I own the air space above it. I am limited in what I am able to build on it and the kind of business I am able to run from it. Several political layers have overlapping claims to my property, each with laws that govern what I can and cannot do. Because I live near a protected wetland, another political layer—in this case, a conservation authority—also governs my relationship with land. I own my land, but so do the city and region, the province and the country. We all have ownership in it, and responsibilities to it, in different ways. And through my property taxes, I pay a kind of tribute to the city. Even if I own my property free and clear, failure to pay that tribute will have my title revoked.

Ownership of land is a social phenomenon, and its purchase embeds you in a web of relationships. Indigenous peoples have long understood this, and our presence on land has meant respecting relationships with human and other-than-human relatives. We understood overlapping claims to the places where we lived, that plants and animals also had claims. We knew that we did not have rights to what lay deep beneath, and we knew that the birds owned the sky. We understood that other tribal groups also had claims, and although we didn't always get along, we also made treaties.

It was into that web of relationships that the Haudenosaunee welcomed the newcomers with the Two Row Wampum. But that was not the kind of relationship that the newcomers had in mind. The settlers turned everything into parcels and products that could be bought and sold and speculated in.

And the Doctrine of Discovery—a bundle of laws and proclamations developed by the church about who had the right to land—meant that they didn't even have to buy it. They could just take it.

※　※　※

In 1621, Massasoit, the leader of a Wampanoag Confederacy, began a relationship with a community of English who had settled in what would become known as New England. By this time, Europeans had been coming and going on the continent for about a hundred years. Some settlements had been more successful than others, and the surrounding Indigenous groups, mostly Wampanoag but also Powhatan and other Algonkian peoples, were learning to manage their presence.

The relationship that Massasoit formed was an alliance with these particular settlers—an agreement that would support him against the Naragansett people to the north, a group with whom the Wampanoag were in frequent conflict. The English would live within Powhatan territory, paying a tribute amount in exchange for land usage; in return, Massasoit could count on them for support. Meanwhile, Roger Williams, another English colonist, made similar agreements with the Naragansetts while he founded the colonies that would become Rhode Island.

At that time, and even today, we did not see ourselves as a unified Indigenous community any more than Europeans saw themselves as a cohesive group. The emerging European states had been fighting among themselves for centuries, as nobles built alliances within what would become nation-state boundaries and then warred against each other. The earliest race theories considered racial differences and hierarchies within Europe itself both in terms of class and racial groups like Anglo Saxon, Celt, and Gaul. Much of the language later used against Indigenous people—words like *wild* and *savage* that questioned our humanity and value—was first used against the Irish when England colonized that island. The English, whose history is rooted in their colonization by ancient Rome, saw themselves as Rome's heirs and better for having been "civilized" by Rome. In their writing and retelling of history, Rome had brought Christianity to the British Isles and, along with it, civilization, and they would do the same for the rest of the world. Whether the rest of the world liked it or not.

Just as European states engaged in conflict over boundaries and resolved these conflicts with various treaties and agreements, Indigenous nations also engaged in conflict and developed models for peace. Among the eastern woodland peoples, these agreements were encoded in wampum belts. Wampum are oblong beads formed from the shells of quahog, or Western North-Atlantic hard-shelled clams. Making these beads, variously purple and white depending on the shading of the shell, was labor intensive, and these large, heavy belts represented a significant investment of time and trade. They served in part as mnemonic devices: not simply images that reflect a single truth but also detailed understandings of the history, reminders of the mutual responsibilities of that treaty. They are a kind of writing that invites participation and evolution—not a once-and-done agreement but a living document whose material expression may change in order to maintain the principles themselves.

The Dish with One Spoon wampum treaty—or One Dish One Spoon, as it is also known—is an agreement between the Haudenosaunee Confederacy and the Anishinaabeg. The bowl represents the land around the St. Lawrence Seaway up into the Ottawa Valley and around both sides of the Great Lakes, reaching into the lands around them. The area described within this treaty is rich in resources. It contains the largest freshwater system on the continent and millions of acres of arable land. Between Lakes Erie and Ontario are micro-climates that permit the growing of grapes and soft fruits well above their typical range. The woodlands sheltered game, and the earliest colonists remarked on it as a paradise.

The treaty, in its simplest terms, requires that those who live in this area share the resources. Although we each had our own villages and followed our own ways, we lived together in this area. The dish has enough for everyone so long as you take only what you need. And it has a spoon, not a knife, suggesting peaceable relations. As with any shared pottery, everyone who uses the bowl is responsible for keeping it clean. This idea of shared place and relationships is found in both the Haudenosaunee concept of the "good mind" and the Anishinaabe principle of the "good life": bimaadiziwin. Both prioritize setting aside ego to focus on relationships and a balanced life.

Allies of these groups were also bound to the agreement. The Treaty of Ghent in 1814 set the boundary between the United States and Canada, but countries that had nothing to do with it still respect that agreement. Other countries that were not signatories to the treaty do not do business in Manitoba, for example, as if they were in Wisconsin. They respect the treaty. So when the colonists arrived and positioned themselves as allies of one group or the other, the Indigenous people expected that they would also respect the principles of the Dish with One Spoon treaty.

In 1613, eight years before Massasoit's arrangement with the English colonists, the Haudenosaunee Confederacy had entered into an agreement with Dutch settlers. This agreement is called the Two Row Wampum treaty and has two purple rows running the length of the belt in between three white rows. The two purple rows represent the two peoples: Haudenosaunee on one side and settler on the other. As we saw in the introduction, the principle of this treaty is that we would travel together but in our own boats, not interfering with each other's politics and communities. The three white rows designated how this relationship would be governed—in peace, friendship, and respect—and that it would be ongoing.

The Dutch recorded this same agreement on paper with the imagery of three silver chains. They chose silver because, while iron can rust and eventually break, silver needs only to be polished; over time, as the relationship tarnishes, the people can gather together again and "polish the chain" to renew relationships. So this agreement is also known as the Silver Covenant Chain of Friendship. As with other treaties, the expectation was that any allies would respect the principles. And as in the Dish with One Spoon treaty that already bound us, we agreed to live in our own ways, without interfering in each other's communities, and to live in peace, friendship, and respect without end.

While the Anishinaabe and Haudenosaunee peoples were developing principles to manage shared space and resources, the Catholic popes were developing their own principles for how to manage shared space. The Doctrine of Discovery was a legal framework of various papal bulls and secular laws that developed over hundreds of years, beginning in the twelfth century. It established spiritual, legal, and political justification for taking land from those who existed outside of the church's influence, other peoples with whom Europeans came into contact. The Doctrine of Discovery said that lands discovered by European powers belonged to those powers because it wasn't owned by Christians.

The lands belonged to the European powers, not individuals. The state would simply lay claim to vast swaths of geography, and individuals would then obtain land from the state. That didn't stop individuals from trying to claim it for themselves, though, and many of them did just that, manipulating the differences in our systems to enrich themselves and dispossess Indigenous peoples.

The British Royal Proclamation of 1763, and then subsequent treaties made between the US and Canadian governments and the Indigenous nations within their borders, established relationships and responsibilities between the state and the Indigenous peoples and relied on the Doctrine of Discovery. In the 1823 ruling *Johnson v. M'Intosh*, the US Supreme Court ruled against a private citizen who had purchased land from a Native American by saying, "The principle of discovery gave *European nations* an absolute right to New World lands." Individuals could not purchase our land from us because the state already owned it.

The insatiable hunger of the US empire—a ravenously hungry big brother who sends out little brothers to bring in more and more—swept across each legal barrier created to contain Indians and keep their land separate from that of the growing colonies. The Doctrine of Discovery still forms the basis for US law even today and indeed the very existence of the American nations. It is the authority by which the European empires claimed ownership of land that was already occupied by sovereign people, something the United States and Canada recognized in their decisions to make treaties with us. Patrick Wolfe describes this in his book *Traces of History*, in which he discusses the treaty process by which the US and Canadian governments dispossessed the Indigenous peoples. This particular process of dispossession, horrific as it is, legitimized them as sovereign groups capable of engaging in a nation-to-nation relationship.

Indigenous nations within American borders continue to point to these treaties as evidence of our sovereignty. This contradiction— the recognition that we were sovereign nations while simultaneously absorbing us into the colonial state—was resolved through that 1823 legal ruling that described the tribes within US borders as "domestic dependent nations." We were sovereign enough to sign treaties but not so sovereign that we were able to refuse the overarching authority of the US government. This fundamental contradiction continues to color processes of consultation and decisions about extraction industries that impact reservation communities. They have an obligation to consult Indigenous communities, but we do not have the power to say no.

The Doctrine of Discovery did not acknowledge Indigenous sovereignty; it simply swept it aside and continues to do so. It was cited as recently as 2005 when the late Supreme Court Justice Ruth Bader Ginsburg wrote the majority decision of a Supreme Court ruling *against* the Oneida nation, who had purchased land to restore a historic reservation. In *City of Sherril v. Oneida Indian Nation of New York*, she wrote, "fee title to the lands occupied by Indians when the colonists arrived became vested in the sovereign—first the discovering European nation and later the original states and the United States." In other words, in accordance with the principles of the Doctrine of Discovery, the 2005 ruling states that the government obtained "fee title" (unrestricted ownership) because they discovered it. And the United States basically inherited the rights associated with discovery when it achieved independence. *The discovering European nation*: sit with that thought for a moment and hear the entitlement invested in those four words.

This principle—that the European states had the right to the land by virtue of finding it—remains the basis for contemporary relationship to land. It gave ownership first to European nations and then to the independent nations that rose from their colonies. It also stands in stark contrast to the treaties of the Haudenosaunee and the Anishinaabeg and the ways that we understood our relationship to land and each other. It wasn't that Indigenous peoples had no concept of land ownership; we understood boundaries and authority. It was that our underlying concepts—the Anishinaabe concept of bimaadiziwin and the Haudenosaunee concept of a good mind—mitigated rather than encouraged the insatiable appetites that transform people into monsters.

Both the Dish with One Spoon and Two Row treaties provided a way for distinct peoples to live together without conflict. They recognized the rights of not only the humans involved in the treaty-making process but also other relatives. Remember that for Indigenous peoples in the Americas, the entire world is alive with people—and not just those of the human variety. Our various traditions speak of treaties made with plant and animal nations, who provided sustenance for us in exchange for care and respect. This hearkens back to our creation story and the belief that we had all collectively promised to take care of each other.

The Hebrew scriptures offer another road than the one taken—an alternate road with which the Christians who modeled themselves after Israel should have been familiar. As the Israelites were preparing to enter the Promised Land, they paused to receive the rules that would govern their lives there, as a matter of sacred duty. These rules are recorded primarily in the book of Leviticus, which contains some intriguing recommendations for this new society. In Leviticus 25, the Hebrew people are told to count off seven years of Sabbaths and that the fiftieth year would be a year of jubilee throughout the land. Rather like the European powers divided the Americas and Africa among them, with no regard for the Indigenous nations already living there, the land of Israel was divided among the tribes with family allotments. They had the ability to buy and sell and to lease and mortgage. But in the fiftieth year, everything reverted back to where it had been. Enslaved people were freed, debts were forgiven, land was restored, and the ledger was wiped free. In this way, families did not accumulate generational wealth, permanently taking more than their share, and if they were impoverished because of poor harvests or poor choices, their children and their grandchildren would get another chance. Land also remained in families, not with individuals, suggesting a more cooperative way of living. Rather than enriching individual members of a family while younger children had to fend for themselves, the entire family was provided for in a way that protected future generations. We see shades of this in the relationship between Boaz and Ruth. Ruth claims a kinship right of support from this wealthy farmer, who had an obligation of care, and in this way, she entered the genealogy of Jesus.

The Bible offers many mechanisms to mitigate the accumulation of wealth. It offers striking examples of generosity and commitment to relationships such as those found in the early church, and it also condemns those who choose wealth and isolate themselves in the face of others' need. When I was studying to be a social worker, I learned about the Catholic Worker movement, a collection of communities formed in 1933 by Dorothy Day and Peter Maurin. They are committed to particular goals around social justice, including hospitality and opposition to war and equality around wealth distribution. Catholic Worker commitment to these ideals includes choosing to live at or below the poverty line so that their taxes don't support military expansion. This forces them to make countercultural choices about how they organize their homes and relationships. Those in the Catholic Worker movement adopt a way of life that prevents the accumulation of wealth and allows them to offer support to those who need it. They choose relationship; they choose a good life.

Many Indigenous nations had mechanisms that prevented the accumulation of wealth, and these mechanisms were forbidden by the US and Canadian governments. From the giveway in the East to the potlatch on the West Coast, Indigenous peoples measured wealth by what was given away. You gave away everything to celebrate a major event, knowing that in the midst of this, your needs would still be met. Just as many did in the book of Acts, Indigenous people would sometimes give everything because they were confident that their community would meet their needs.

Wealth is inevitably held in the hands of the few, brought to the insatiably hungry big brother by those he has enslaved. The question remains: When will the little brother finally stand up and say "enough"?

## Aambe

When the colonists arrived and as settlement moved across the continent, agreements were made. Some were simple like the alliance between the Wampanoag chief and the community of English who settled nearby, or the Two Row. There were peace and friendship treaties made throughout the Atlantic colonies. These would be followed by more formal agreements that were signed and witnessed. In the late 1800s, the US frontier was declared closed, and any further agreements were made through legislation. In Canada, they simply stopped making treaties by the time they got to British Columbia. Using a website like Native Land Digital (https://native-land.ca/), find out which treaties govern the relationships with Indigenous people in your city or state. Using that as a starting point, what can you find out about promises that were made and forgotten?

This website is also a good resource that allows you to search much of the Americas, Pacifica, and Northern Europe for information on territories, languages, and treaties.

# CHAPTER 3

# REMOVAL: BACKGROUND NOISE

During elementary school, I watched the film *Paddle to the Sea*. An Ojibwe boy carves a wooden model of a man in a canoe with the words "Please put me back in the water. I am Paddle-to-the-Sea" on the bottom. He sets it in the snow, which melts into the streams and creeks that carry the carving to Lake Nipigon, about sixty miles north of Lake Superior. Paddle-to-the-Sea makes his way down the Nipigon River to Lake Superior, then through each of the Great Lakes in turn, and eventually up the St. Lawrence Seaway to the Atlantic Ocean. There, the little wooden man in the canoe is picked up in the fishing nets of a French trawler and taken across the ocean to France. Along the way, Paddle-to-the-Sea gets stuck in various obstacles and is rescued by various people, who inscribe on him the places where they picked him up and return him to the water.

I was fascinated by this story that was about me and yet not. The boy isn't identified as Ojibwe; I am inferring that from the location. The area around Lake Nipigon is Anishinaabe territory, and in that area, the people are mostly Ojibwe Anishinaabe. As a child, I knew that's where my father's people were from, even though I didn't yet know them. In the book, he is just an Indian boy without a name, and the story isn't really about him, although it circles back to him at the end. Paddle-to-the-Sea makes it to France, and eventually a newspaper article is written about the carving and all the places it has been. The Indian boy is a grown man by this time, working as a fishing or hunting guide, an anonymous Indian doing anonymous Indian work. He sees the newspaper article but doesn't draw any attention to himself as the carver of the boat.

The film, made by the National Film Board of Canada in 1966, is based on the 1941 book by Holling C. Holling. The story is based in stereotype, and the main character is a carving, not a person. Holling C. Holling is from Michigan, where the Odawa, Pottawatomi, Mississauga, and Ojibwe, all of whom are Anishinaabeg, live around the north and south shores of the Great Lakes that border this state. He was surrounded by places with Anishinaabe names, including the name of the state itself. *Mishigami*, the Ojibwe word from which "Michigan" comes, means "large water" or "large lake." But how many people know this? Like the Indian boy of this story, we and our words are background noise.

Many of our provinces and states, our cities and rivers, are words in native languages. I live in Chippewa, a town along the Niagara River. The cities of Mississauga and Toronto are nearby. I live in Canada, and our capital city is Ottawa. We have provinces named Ontario, Manitoba, Saskatchewan, and Alberta, just as the United States has states named Alabama, Idaho, Hawaii, Arizona, Connecticut, and more. I have cruised on the Chicago River and embarrassed myself singing about the Tallahatchie at karaoke. Washington crossed the Delaware, and I've driven over the Mississippi. They are part of our everyday vocabulary, yet they are ambient sounds that fill in the silence and that no one really notices.

These new countries pushed us aside just as ancient glaciers had done, leaving behind pebbles of names and barren communities in a new landscape dominated by new peoples. There is no such thing as wilderness, writes Patrick Wolfe in *Traces of History*—only depopulation.

The story of colonization is one of displacement, of disruption, of ghosts left behind and of those who make flutes of their bones. The early colonists made deals for land, paying tribute and living in often uneasy peace with their Indigenous neighbors, but this period did not last. As we saw in the last chapter, European hunger for land was insatiable. They just kept coming.

For four hundred years, settlers swarmed over the continent, following waterways and trails they carved into mountains. They burned across the prairie like a wildfire consuming the deep-rooted grasses and leaving thirsty crops like wheat and corn in their wake. Creative and innovative, they used whatever strategies they could to push us aside. The missionaries often came first, then traders and settlers, all with the protection of the military and laws that justified theft and displacement. By the late nineteenth century, the West was won. Manifest Destiny rested on Enlightenment beliefs about correct land use, racial hierarchies, and a certainty that their authority was derived from ancient roots, if not from God himself.

※　※　※

Thousands of years ago, Aristotle believed that the temperate climate of the Mediterranean created superior people. The barbarians to the north and the Black people to the south were less evolved, he thought, because their climates were either too hot or too cold to promote true civilization. Thus, he began to connect race and slavery. In her book *The History of White People*, Nell Irvin Painter notes that the word *slave* comes from the Slavic peoples who were some of Aristotle's northern barbarians, many of whom were among those enslaved throughout the Middle Ages. So it is true that for a time white people were also enslaved, as were the Irish, who were not considered white until fairly recently. But that is not the slavery that built the Americas.

A slave trade existed in the early modern period, largely operated by Muslim traders, and for hundreds of years before the Portuguese slave trade, there were enslaved Africans in China. Muslim presence in Europe and around the Mediterranean was such that from the eighth century CE, the southern part of the Iberian Peninsula, what is now Spain, was controlled by North African Muslims, the Moors. For hundreds of years, wars would be fought while Christian kingdoms expanded across Europe. In his book *Praying to the West*, Omar Mouallem describes the presence of Christians and Jews within Moorish Spain as one of importance and mutual respect, but in 1492, the same year that Columbus set sail, Granada fell, and the Iberian Peninsula was Christian. These conquests, in Europe, Africa, and the Americas, set in motion a white Christian supremacy that remains visible in the violence done to mosques and synagogues, as well as the violence done to Black and Indigenous peoples.

It was in this context that the Portuguese obtained from the pope the exclusive rights to the slave trade on the west coast of Africa. This was a political and economic decision rooted in anti-Muslim sentiment, and it would eventually enrich the Portuguese and Spanish crowns by providing a vast unfree labor force with which to extract wealth from the lands that Columbus "discovered." A primarily African labor force that was likely one-third Muslim.

The Doctrine of Discovery entitled Christian explorers not only to land but to *people*, as long as the people they found weren't already Christians. These twin entitlements—to land and to bodies—formed the basis for the nations of the Western Hemisphere. These nations are built on stolen land and displaced people.

Background noise.

Years ago, I heard a sermon about the Babylonian exile. The passage was 2 Kings 24:12–17, and it describes Nebuchadnezzar, the king of Babylon, laying siege to Jerusalem and then taking the treasures and the people back to Babylon, carrying away soldiers and artisans, craftspeople and royalty. Nebuchadnezzar left behind only the poorest people and replaced King Jehoiachin with Jehoiachin's nephew Mattaniah.

As the pastor recounted the long walk from Israel to Babylon—a distance of between seven hundred and nine hundred miles, depending on your route—he asked us to imagine what that must have been like: the invasion of your cities and communities by the army. The frantic collection of whatever you could carry. The search for family members in the gathered crowds. Then the march over mountains and into deserts, looking over your shoulder while home recedes in the distance, every step taking you farther away and into exile.

"Imagine," the preacher said. "Can you imagine?"

Yes, I wanted to say in that moment. I can imagine.

Imagine.

Imagine my friend Twila, the first generation of her family born into a non-Cherokee-speaking household. Imagine her mother, Clara, going to an Indian boarding school where the language she spoke from birth was stolen from her. Clara was the daughter of Aaron, who was the son of Nancy, who received her land allotment and US citizenship at eighteen months. Nancy is the daughter of

Johnson Jr., the son of Johnson Sr., who served in the Cherokee Nation government and in the US Army during the Civil War. Johnson Sr. is the son of Hatchet. Imagine Hatchet forced to leave everything behind. Imagine his wife, Betsy, a white woman, dying and being buried along the way. Imagine this journey from north-central Georgia through Alabama, Mississippi, and Arkansas to the eastern edge of Oklahoma: some seven hundred miles, known as the Trail of Tears.

The Trail of Tears was the most well-known removal of the Cherokee from Georgia to Indian Territory. Yet it is only one of several removals that took place in the 1830s, an ethnic cleansing of the lands east of the Mississippi. Clearing these states not only freed thousands of acres for plantations and led directly to the rise of King Cotton but removed Indigenous tribes who often acted as allies for escaped slaves. More than one hundred thousand Indigenous peoples were removed from the eastern seaboard, replaced by enslaved Africans whose labor enriched those at the top of the social hierarchy. Later, in the clearing of the West, the US government would use Buffalo Soldiers, who were Black, ensuring that the first meetings between Plains tribes and African Americans was under much different circumstances than that of earlier meetings, when many eastern tribes gave shelter to those fleeing slavery. This same principle of removal of people and seizure of land, which eventually consumed the land all the way to the Pacific Ocean, would be applied to Japanese Americans under the pretext of protecting the nation after the attacks on Pearl Harbor. Their farmlands were seized while they were interred. Lands they once cared for now enriched white farmers and corporate agriculture.

These multiple trails of tears crossed the Appalachian Mountains in winter and resulted in thousands of deaths just like Betsy's. From the

Cherokee in the South to the Pottawatomi in the North to dozens of tribal groups in between, thousands were forced to walk into captivity. Andrew Jackson's Indian Removal Act legislated the removal of Indians from dozens of tribes in the land east of the Mississippi. In addition to harboring escaped slaves, many in the so-called Five Civilized Tribes—the Cherokee, Choctaw, Chickasaw, Creek, and Seminole—had become slave owners. And so when they were forced west of the Mississippi, the Black people in their communities, the free and enslaved, went with them. And just as Twila's ancestor Hatchet brought his wife, Betsy, white spouses and family members also went with them. Scattered reservations exist throughout the original thirteen states, but because of these removals—this ethnic cleansing of the eastern seaboard—the vast majority of reservations are west of the Mississippi.

Indigenous peoples did not willingly leave their homes, and there was, of course, resistance to the forced removal. An alliance between the Seminole and Black people who had fled slavery fought incursions by white settlers and against removal for decades in the Everglades, which became known as the Seminole Wars. They eventually reached a settlement for safe passage to what was then called Indian Country. Some Cherokee leaders, with their people starving and under constant threat of violence, signed a treaty that agreed to their removal. Not everyone left. Small groups of people can hide when they know the territory, and the geography of the southeastern United States was well known to them.

The land to which the eastern tribes were removed—the land that the US government designated as "Indian Country"—was not empty. The southern plains were home to the Caddo Confederacy and the Kichai people long before the nineteenth century. The Kiowa, Apache, and Comanche people had moved in, pushed out of their lands by the Spanish as they moved their empire north. The

Quapaw and Osage had also moved in, ahead of eastern colonization. Exiles and refugees, pushed aside by the needs of the growing
country, made homes among those who were already there.

Africans were also moved: first as captives taken from their inland
homes and marched to various West Coast ports, and then across the
Atlantic Ocean on the Middle Passage, where thousands died from
sickness and desperation without setting foot on land. They landed
in the Caribbean and in cities up and down the Atlantic seaboard.
Unlike settlers, who stopped to work in one place before choosing
to move to another in search of land, enslaved people are forcibly *displanted*, that term coined by human rights lawyer Anthony
Morgan to describe the experience of Africans in diaspora. They
were uprooted and replanted again and again from one location to
another, depending on someone else's need and without regard for
the relationships that they formed. Husbands were separated from
wives, parents from children. At times, the movement was done
simply to sever relationships, to prevent community from developing. This persists even today. Highways often bisect communities
of color, housing projects are slated for redevelopment, and tenants
relocated temporarily only to find that they can't afford their newly
renovated homes. The term *environmental racism* was coined in the
1970s to capture this pattern of locating industrial processing, waste
storage, incinerators, and bridges near primarily Black and Indigenous neighborhoods and lands.

My friend Kerry is the daughter of Joslyn, a nurse who moved her
family to England and then Canada in search of a home and stabil-
ity. Joslyn was born on the island of Antigua. Her father, Reginald,
was also born in Antigua, where he worked. Reginald never spoke
of his father, Kerry's great-grandfather, who was born in Haiti and
skilled in voudon.

And that's where the names stop: with an unnamed great-grandfather who was born in Haiti and whose relatives surely came from somewhere. They were listed on bills of sale and cargo manifests as "negro male" and "mulatto girl." Counted and weighed but not always named.

The story of America as a nation of proud immigrants is a myth, one that Roxanne Dunbar-Ortiz unpacks in her book *Not "A Nation of Immigrants."* Put simply, immigrants come to a place and join with the existing political order. Settlers come to a place and impose a political order. Those who came here by force—such as African people who were enslaved—or those who come through desperation—such as economic or climate refugees or those fleeing war—are welcomed by that political order only according to their usefulness. Those seen as threats are contained in prisons and migrant detention centers, just as Native people were contained in reservations. The United States has never been "a nation of immigrants." The Haudenosaunee offered settlers a kind of immigration—a way to join with the existing political order through the Two Row Wampum. Instead, the United States chose to become a settler-colonial nation, imposing a new order.

Natives, Africans, Europeans, and more all have migration stories. We all moved. We moved across oceans and land. But there is a profound difference between moving and being moved. Between being welcomed and being used.

In the early colonial period, there was a short-lived experiment, between 1643 and 1675, in which Puritan leaders in Massachusetts and Jesuit missionaries in Quebec organized what they called

praying towns. These were an attempt to control the local Indigenous people and convert them by separating them from their often
mobile communities and have them settle near the colonists. Natives
who agreed to live in these towns got financial assistance, education,
religious instruction, and jobs. After the defeat of the Narragansett,
Wampanoag, and many other smaller tribes, the balance of power
shifted, missionaries turned their attentions to other frontiers, and
the missionary aspect of these towns faded. They became Indian settlements, municipal towns and villages similar to the communities
of Alaska Natives or the Inuit of northern Canada.

Reservations, which were created in 1851 by the Indian Appropri-
ations Act, had clearly defined borders. Native people did not become
US citizens until 1924. In Canada, we were gradually enfranchised,
losing our Indian status if we went to university or fought in the military, and it wasn't until 1960 that we stopped being "wards of the
Crown" and became Canadian citizens. But in the nineteenth century in the United States and Canada, Indians retained their tribal
identity, and the federal government agreed to provide support in
cash and food in exchange for the land that was relinquished. I sus-
pect that these provisions were also intended to keep us contained,
to ensure that we did not leave the lines drawn around us. The size of
the reservation was often calculated based on the number of Indians.
Just as large tracts of land were divided up into plots to be given to
settler families, certain acreages were designated for Indian families.
So government officials would count the number of families in a
tribal group and give them what they thought was an appropriate
number of acres. That would form the basis of the reservation, and
the rest of the land could then be given away to settler families.

Unlike Indian towns, where land was held privately and often
fell out of Indian hands, reservation land was not accessible to

settlers—and settlers wanted land. So legislators soon developed a few strategies to make it accessible. One was to simply move the entire tribe to a new location, as Andrew Jackson did with the Indian Removal Act that authorized the Trail of Tears. That freed up thousands of acres for settlers east of the Appalachian Mountains. But there's only so much land a growing country can relocate people *to*, so another solution was offered: allotment. The process of allotment would come to devastate the tribes involved.

When Senator Henry Dawes visited the Cherokee Nation in Oklahoma decades after their removal, he found them to be thriving. This surprised him. They had a school, hospital, and bicameral system of governance. Nobody did without. According to Dawes, this was socialism. There was, he said, "no incentive to make your home better than that of your neighbor. There is no selfishness, which is at the bottom of civilization." This propensity for collective ownership confounded settlers, who understood the buying and selling of land as the basis of wealth and civilization. The Dawes Act was their solution. It broke up reservations and divided Indian Country—that land west of the Mississippi to which Andrew Jackson had marched dozens of tribes—into allotments. Those allotments were then distributed to tribal citizens as individuals rather than as tribal groups.

Imagine a checkerboard. Under the reservation system, the land that was set aside for Indians was collected together, in one place, with the intention that it would remain as a single piece of federally owned property on which tribal members could live. Indian land would be all the squares on one side of the board, and settlers would have the other side. Under allotment, however, the land that was set aside for Indians was broken up into smaller squares—land that settlers could now buy. Those squares got snapped up pretty quickly, leaving Indians with scattered blocks. This broke up communities and families. Land that was allotted to Indians became the target of scams and deals that promised wealth and delivered poverty and dispossession.

These allotments were also given on the basis of blood quantum, that strange calculus that determines what percentage Indian you are based on your parents and grandparents. If you were mostly white, you owned your land outright. If you were mostly Indian, it was held in trust for twenty-five years while you learned how to manage land.

Blood quantum is a race theory that still forms the basis for legal Indian status in the United States and Canada. So we have to back up a bit and talk about race.

❋    ❋    ❋

Long before they knew there was a new world, Europeans had ideas about race connected to the rights you had in society: whether you were an owner or the owned. Within medieval European society, there were peasants and nobles, and today we would likely classify both groups as "white." But given the complexities of race in Europe, they did not. In her book *The History of White People*, Nell Irvin Painter describes how, over time, ideas about who was white eventually came to include all Europeans. But it did not start out that way.

The Europeans arrived in the new world with expectations guided by Aristotle's climate theory on race. But even in the hottest climates, we were not as dark as they expected us to be, so like good scientists, they adjusted their theory. It was no longer about climate; it was about development and civilization. They adjusted their color-coded hierarchy to include "red" people. Eventually the categories would include Asians, designated "yellow," and then Malaysians, who were "brown."

In this new way of organizing the world, when you separate people from land, all you are left with to distinguish difference is race. Willie James Jennings makes this point in *The Christian Imagination*, in which he talks about the early theologians' attempts to fit the new world into their Christian theology. The Christian world began in the Middle East and fanned out from there, disconnected from the place of its birth, uprooted and unmoored. Christians are identified by their beliefs, not their place. But when I say that I am Anishinaabe, I am not only making a claim to who I am; I am making a claim to a place. I am claiming a land that claims me back. When I say that I am Ojibwe Anishinaabe, I am making an even more specific claim. I am claiming the lands from where Paddle-to-the-Sea began his journey. When my mother says she is Ukrainian, she is also making a claim to place. But when you disconnect people from place—when they become white or Black or Indian—there is no longer any such claim.

In order to gain access to the land of my ancestors, the colonists needed to separate us from it, to make it not-ours. Settlers needed to make us Indians instead of Anishinaabe, which is why these broad terms can be so fraught. In order to enslave Africans, enslavers needed to separate them from their land, and in that way the ancestors of my friends stopped being Igbo or Yoruba and became Black.

Race is not biologically real, not in the sense that you can tell somebody's race by testing their blood or measuring their skull. It's a social construct, like marriage and citizenship: an idea that got mapped onto humans, replacing relationships with identity and then attaching rights to that identity—rights like who could own land and who could be owned. But people don't stay in tidy racial categories. People get married. People get raped. Skin color becomes an increasingly unreliable way to decide who belongs in which part of the city and in which kinds of work. So race, like marriage and citizenship, became defined legally.

Beginning in the eighteenth century and into the early decades of the twentieth, there were laws throughout the United States regarding race. Depending on the state, a person could be legally white if three grandparents or seven great-grandparents were white. It wasn't until after the Civil War, when slavery was no longer available to keep white and Black separate, that the "one drop rule," a principle meant to address "invisible Blackness," began to be adopted in law. In 1924, the Racial Integrity Act in the state of Virginia defined a person as legally Black if they had *any* African ancestry. This was also the act with the so-called Pocahontas exception: if you had Native American ancestry, you could still be considered legally white.

Do you see what happened there? One Black ancestor and the whole family is Black. One Native ancestor and you're still white. Why? Because a country whose economy relied on slavery and land always needed slaves more than it needed Indians. In *Traces of History*, Patrick Wolfe describes a global process of removing Native people from land to create space for white settlement and then enslaving them elsewhere to support that settlement. Concepts of race are malleable and strategic, always benefiting those in power. A particular understanding of race allowed Americans to increase the population of those they wanted to continue enslaving and to erase the population of those they wanted to disappear.

※　※　※

So to get back to reservations and allotment: if all four of your grandparents were believed to be Cherokee, then you were considered a "full blood." If only two of your grandparents were believed to be

Cherokee, then you were a "half blood." This kind of blood math has created some strange designations for contemporary Indians. People can have tribal ID cards that read: 12.5 percent Choctaw, 25 percent Lakota, 50 percent Ojibwe, with the remainder being considered white or not Native.

When the government looks at those numbers, it is concerned with how they add up. Do they add up to 50 percent Indian? More? Less? Do we have an obligation to this person? Or is the number low enough that they're practically white? When the government looks at those numbers, it is looking for disconnection, a way out of its responsibilities, a way to get us off what remains of our land. When we look at those numbers, we see relatives, connections to people and places. A Choctaw great-grandmother. A Lakota grandfather. An Ojibwe parent.

What's even stranger about these numbers, as I noted, is that many times these designations were initially based on what the government's representative at the time of allotment *believed* about your parentage. They made determinations about full or half blood based on what they thought and how you looked, less on who your parents actually were.

Many Black Natives were erased completely. Remember that having a Black parent meant you were Black, regardless of how many white ancestors you had. Black was a legal category, and it applied to the children of Black and Native people as well. The children of these relationships were often identified as Black on birth records, despite having a Native parent. This had consequences for citizenship in tribal nations and social consequences in terms of belonging that many tribes are still working out today.

This also had consequences for land allocated to tribes. In the 1800s, just as the reservations were forming, Black people were not permitted to own property. Any property owned by a Black person was subject to confiscation, and so some tribes rejected their Black relatives in order to preserve their diminishing land holdings. Colonialism destroys in order to replace. And it destroyed our relationships with each other.

Anyone with less than 50 percent blood quantum was given their land outright because they were considered capable of using land in the "correct" way. Those considered "full bloods," or nearly full bloods, had their allotments held in trust; they were seen as still "too Indian" to be trusted to manage their lands independently and needed federal supervision. So their land would be held in trust for twenty-five years, at which point they were allowed to sell it. The rest of the land in the area subject to allotment was then made available to settlers, who had to meet various criteria to complete their land claim. They often failed to meet those criteria, and the land was taken up by corporations and agricultural businesses.

Allotment took place after the Civil War, when free Blacks were moving out of the South. Many of them came to Oklahoma, where communities with businesses and jobs had emerged around the lands allotted to freedmen—communities like Greenwood, a neighborhood in Tulsa that would later be the location of the Tulsa Race Massacre.

Indian Territory was the formal designation for that land west of the Mississippi, which was promised to the Cherokee and others for "as long as the river flows and the grass grows," a phrase often used by government agents to promise the everlasting nature of treaties. Indian Territory was dissolved in 1907, along with the reservations within what would become the state of Oklahoma.

Folk singer and songwriter Woody Guthrie grew up in Oklahoma, and a lot of Native people hear the words of his anthem "This

Land Is Your Land" in this context. When Guthrie sings that this "land is your land, this land is my land," he isn't singing about me. The history of his hometown is the history of the grift that happened after allotment. Okemah, Oklahoma, was incorporated in 1902 and named for a Kickapoo chief who lived near there at the time. The land that Okemah sat on had been allotted to Mahala and Nocus Fixico. Fixico was a full-blood Mvskoke Creek, which under the terms of the Dawes Act meant that he shouldn't have been able to sell his land for twenty-five years. But the Department of the Interior wanted the land for a town, and they disregarded their own legislation so they could buy it. This kind of corruption was rampant, as millions of acres were at stake. This land was my land, but now it's your land.

Settlers who wanted land during the allotment period often made spurious claims to being Creek, or Seminole, or Cherokee in order to get an allotment or control over an Indian child and the land allotted to the child. These spurious claims became family myths, and even today people will say that they are "part Indian" as an entitlement to belonging. But this kind of claim to being Indian isn't about belonging to a community; it works to erase us, to shift us off the land and replace us with white settlers who are "part Indian."

Remember Twila's great-grandmother Nancy? She received her allotment when she was eighteen months old, and so it was held in trust for her, most likely by her grandmother Polly, who raised her. This was fortunate for Nancy. If someone had control of a Cherokee child, then they had control over that child's allotment—and that was a powerful motivation for fraud and dispossession.

The Indian Reorganization Act of 1934 put a stop to allotment, which had devastated tribal holdings throughout the Great Plains, not only in Oklahoma. Yet while the act was intended to undo some of the harms of allotment, it also imposed a system of governance on the American Indians who remained. Our systems of governance must have baffled the colonists and then the Americans. Although there was diversity across the continent and varying degrees of organization, for the most part, our governance operated in horizontal rather than vertical structures, with a plurality of leadership and consensus model of decision-making. And while the tribes recognized by the federal government were able to put together their own constitutions, those constitutions had to include a kind of government like those of settler towns and cities. When traditional people in some tribes insisted on their own traditional ways, their constitutions were rejected. This had consequences in terms of funding and recognition and whether the government would later be willing to hear from you regarding projects like dams that directly impacted your tribe.

Remember Israel's march into captivity? The narrator tells us that the king of Babylon put somebody he liked in charge of what remained. So did the US government. Through the Indian Reorganization Act in the United States and the Indian Act in Canada, governments have imposed not only a kind of leadership that makes sense to them but one that undermines our communities and forces hierarchies of power where they didn't exist before. That has led to conflicts and corruption in some tribal governments just as we see in American governments.

It is normal to see ourselves in these histories recorded in the Bible, but it is important to think about *how* we see ourselves and in whom. Too often the descendants of European Christians see themselves as persecuted Israelites rather than as members of the invading state of Babylon: an empire that imposes systems of oppressive leadership over the people of the land for the purpose of control and prosperity.

❊    ❊    ❊

In the early 1800s, James Fenimore Cooper wrote the fictional series "The Leatherstocking Tales." In doing so, the man Herbert Melville called "our national novelist" created the myth of America. His hero, Natty Bumpo, starts on the East Coast and moves west, experiencing the foundational stories of America, from the French and Indian Wars to wagon trains, in a way that was very flattering to the emerging American people who had just achieved independence and needed a creation story. In Cooper's book *The Last of the Mohicans*, set in 1757, Natty, a British soldier, is adopted by the Mohican Chingachgook. Chingachgook is a pure and noble Indian who dies after entrusting the new frontier to Natty, who has been given the Indian name Hawkeye.

The Mohicans have not vanished. They were relocated to Wisconsin during the removals of the 1820s and 1830s. People continue to be surprised by that fact because the myth of the vanishing Indian is such an enduring part of American history. From Cooper to Daniel Boone to *Little House on the Prairie*, Native peoples are pushed aside and replaced by the new Americans. A relentless ethnic cleansing that began on the East Coast and moved westward as big brother's hunger for land and resources grew ever more demanding. The US invasion of Mexico in 1846 resulted in the acquisition of almost half of the current US territory. The gold rush in California brought the forty-niners, miners who, despite the romanticized history that has grown up around them, were brutally violent. Later expansions would continue into Alaska and Hawaii, Guam and the Philippines.

Manifest Destiny, a phrase coined in 1845 by a newspaper editor, is the idea that God had ordained the expansion of Christian settlement throughout the continent. It reached across the Pacific and into Central America the same way that the Doctrine of Discovery reached across the Atlantic. This continental expansion of the United States followed the familiar pattern of removal and replacement.

Church missions either led the way or moved into the aftermath of the colonization, to convert and "save" traumatized people. A number of years ago, I went to San Antonio, Texas, to see the missions. They are sobering places. The information plaques tell stories of safety and refuge, describing them as places where Native tribes could come for safety from marauding Kiowa or Apache. Those plaques didn't tell the stories of abuse or why tribes that had found a way to live at peace with each other were now warring again. The plaques didn't talk about the mission's own slavery and land theft or the beating and starving of Indigenous people who refused to convert. The plaques were as whitewashed as the buildings.

Almost one hundred years after Cooper's *The Last of the Mohicans* vanished us from the eastern woodlands, another vanishing took place. This happened on the other side of the continent when Ishi, who came to be called the "last wild Indian," died. Although there are still many tribal groups in California today, Ishi was the last known member of the Yahi people. The Yahi community was attacked in what is called the Three Knolls Massacre in 1865, after the gold rush brought tens of thousands to California in search of gold and into conflict with the people already living there.

The survivors of that attack, Ishi and his family among them, fled into the hills and went into hiding. Then one day in 1911, Ishi came out of the hills, alone. He was befriended by two anthropologists, Alfred Louis Kroeber and Thomas Waterman, who took him to the Museum of Anthropology. There, he was given a place to live and work as a janitor until his death in 1916. His name, Ishi, means "man" in the Yana language.

That name was given to him by one of the anthropologists. When they asked what his name was, he said that he had none, as there were no people to name him.

## Aambe

What or whom are the places around you named for?

Adam's first task was to name things. In the Anishinaabe creation story, Nanabush has this task, walking the earth and naming what he finds. The colonists did this as well but in reverse. They *unnamed* the places they came to, sometimes replacing our words with names more familiar to them. Other times, settlers left our words as echoes of people who are no longer seen. Names are never neutral; they have something to teach us about our history and how we see ourselves in a place. They create a relationship.

Notice the names around you: the places and buildings, the streets and rivers. Google the names of places that intrigue you or are so familiar you barely notice them anymore.

What is the history of the names that surround you?

# CHAPTER 4

# REPLACEMENT: THE VANISHING INDIAN

There are many ways for Indigenous peoples to disappear.

Through various proclamations, treaties, and removals, we disappeared from the land and into towns and Indian Country and finally reservations. We disappeared in fiction and film, becoming two-dimensional characters, populating shows from the *Lone Ranger* to the *X Files*, who either threaten white settlement or, like Tonto, exist only to help the white man. We disappear in songs about land that was made for you but not me. The prevailing story about Indians is about our vanishing, sad but inevitable. That belief has consequences that we will explore in this chapter, because despite the myth of the vanishing Indian, we have not completely disappeared.

Our collective identities remained centered around land that no longer lay beneath our feet but remained in our memories. The land persists, and so do we. We may not have been home, but we knew where home was, and our creation stories tell us how to live in new places. How to sink roots deep into the earth, roots that would find their way home and connect us in ways that are unseen and yet felt.

The tribes that had been removed from east of the Mississippi made new homes and new relationships. We were all moved and relocated according to the needs of this new colonial state, and despite

this, we all found new ways to root ourselves collectively in these
new places. Language and religious beliefs and practices remained
and connected our diasporic communities to each other and to new
relatives. New frontiers, those liminal spaces between cultures where
people overlap, forged new relationships and sometimes new conflicts. Having separated us from the land of our creation, the United
States and Canada would develop new strategies to separate us from
each other. In the late nineteenth century, new strategies emerged—
ones that carried well into the twentieth century and whose impacts
persist today.

By the late 1800s, most Indians, those whose tribes were recognized by state or federal governments, had disappeared from the
American landscape into their reservations. It would not be long
before their children would disappear too—taken from those reservations into federally funded and mandated boarding schools.

In 1891, a new law allowed US government officials to forcibly
remove Native children from their homes and send them to residential schools. Between 1894 and 1947, Canadian law required Native
children to attend these schools. Parents who refused could be jailed,
but most often they were simply overpowered and their children
taken away.

Every American Indian in the United States and Canada has
been touched by the residential school system in one way or another.
The generational trauma that resulted from decades of this policy
is incalculable. There is the loss of language and stories, the loss of
relationship. There is the deliberate forgetting of our personal histories to avoid the pain of not forgetting. This destruction of what
was ours replaced our languages with French, English, and Spanish;
our stories with the Bible; and our systems of kinship with isolated
nuclear families.

These losses have been woven into our existence as Native people, written into our DNA as surely as our ancestors are.

❋   ❋   ❋

To be a "person" in the United States and Canada is to be a particular kind of person: somebody who is white and Christian, owns property, holds European values. We may think that this is no longer true today. But 98 percent of private property, 856 million acres of it, in the United States is still owned by white Americans. In fact, just five white people own nine million acres of rural property, which is one million more than all Black Americans own combined. There are about fifty-five million acres in the United States that exist as reservations, but Native people only own eleven million of those acres; the United States owns the balance. Property ownership, European values, Christianity: these were the things that Senator Dawes felt were lacking among the Cherokee in Oklahoma before he brought in the allotment process, and these were the things that Brigadier General Richard Henry Pratt sought to instill in the American Indians through the education of their children.

Pratt had served in the Union Army, and in 1875, he transported seventy-two captive Cheyenne Indians to Fort Marion, Florida. He held them there, and during this period of captivity, he transformed them: he cut their hair, dressed them in military clothes, and drilled them daily. Pratt developed what would become the goal of the entire network of Indian residential schools: "kill the Indian, save the man." Four years later, in 1879, he would found the Carlisle Indian Industrial School, the first Indian boarding school in the United States.

Indian boarding schools were an attempt by the governments of the United States and Canada to change the language, religion, and social structure of Indigenous societies and homogenize everyone into the same way of thinking and living. Although these schools predate the UN Genocide Convention by over fifty years, they meet the criteria of that definition of genocide.

*Genocide* is a legal term that emerged in the aftermath of World War II. The UN Genocide Convention—adopted by the member countries in 1948 but not ratified by the United States until 1988—defines the crime of genocide as "any of the following acts committed with the intent to destroy, in whole or in part, a national, ethnical, racial, or religious group as such:

(a)   Killing members of the group;
(b)   Causing serious bodily or mental harm to members of the group;
(c)   Deliberately inflicting on the group conditions of life calculated to bring about its physical destruction in whole or in part;
(d)   Imposing measures intended to prevent births within the group;
(e)   Forcibily transferring children of the group to another group"

The participation of people with good intentions doesn't change a system that exists to cause harm. In fact, the participation of good people ensures its success. In the United States and Canada, Christian denominations were funded by the government to create schools on and near Indian reservations. Most of these schools were run by the Catholic Church, but that does not absolve other denominations that only had a few of these schools or none at all.

These schools—along with churches, policing, and child welfare—worked together to create a particular world. Christians, especially white Christians, were safe and comfortable in that world, even if they might have disliked the methods used by others to create it. It was, after all, the existence of these schools and the destruction of Indigenous communities that made way for the towns and cities where white people could settle—towns and cities that often bear the names of displaced Native tribes. Governments in the Global South still rely on churches to educate the poorest children, and the same churches that ran residential schools now fund schools in other countries.

The Mohawk Institute, founded in 1828, was run by the Anglican Church in the city of Brantford, Ontario, and is just outside the Canadian reserve Six Nations of the Grand River. Considered to be the first residential school to operate in Canada, it remained in operation until 1970. These schools multiplied by the hundreds across the United States and in Canada. Off-reserve education of children was mandatory in the United States until 1978, and although most of the schools have closed, a few remain open. In Canada, the last government-run boarding school closed in 1996, the same year that the Fresh Prince left Bel Air.

The Mohawk Institute is now the Woodland Cultural Center, providing space for tours, art installations, and a museum that tells the story of residential schools in Canada more broadly. When I was working in child welfare, college students who were studying for their social-work degrees would sometimes accompany me on home visits. One day, I took a student with me to an appointment with a family living on Six Nations of the Grand River, a reserve about ninety minutes from my home. There is a link between residential schools and child welfare, as we will see in this chapter, and I wanted this history to be real for him, so we went to what had once been the Mohawk Institute. As we arrived, a tour was starting, and so we slipped in and spent the next two hours walking through the large brick building with a tour group.

The first stop was a room off the front entryway with a glass window. This was the room where parents could come and visit their children. For the first month, there would be no visits, our guide explained; the staff believed the child needed time to settle in before being disrupted by the parents' visit. Once visits were permitted, one hour per month, they took place in this room. The children and parents had to speak English so that the staff who observed the visit could understand what was said. As our group moved on, I lingered a bit. The child welfare office where I worked at the time had small rooms. With glass windows. Where parents and children would visit.

We moved as a group, room by room, while the guide relayed stories that had been shared with the institute by those who had attended this school as children. We looked at the large spaces that had been dormitory rooms, where children had slept, divided by age and gender. These divisions separated siblings and cousins, further isolating the children from their relatives. We walked through the kitchen, where the children prepared meals for staff from the fruits and vegetables that they labored to grow. Then we went into the dining hall, where the children ate the mush that gave the school its colloquial name: the Mush Hole. We stopped in the basement, where priests would instigate and then bet on fights between the boys. We heard stories of fights that went "too far" and of children who didn't return to their beds.

One story about the Mush Hole that I have heard several times is about the orchard: that trees were planted after children went missing as a way of hiding unmarked graves. I often think about the roots of those trees, encircling these lost children with care. I think of the teachers and visiting dignitaries eating their fruit.

Photographs of residential schools show children kneeling on or beside their beds in a posture of prayer, shorn heads staring up at the camera from their schoolwork, a large cross always hanging on the wall behind them. As with Pratt's experiment on Native captives, the children's hair was cut upon arrival to these schools. Hair is significant in every culture. The way we that we think about hair— covered or uncovered, long or short—is never neutral. When these children had their hair cut, it was an act of violence, the first step in taking the Indian out of the child.

The rooms of the Mohawk Institute seemed profoundly sad, each one a container for grief and loss. For me, the lounge where the children watched television in the later years of the school felt deeply personal. I knew that children were sitting in this very lounge in 1970, when I was at home watching the same TV shows that they probably watched: *Bonanza* and *Lassie*, *Star Trek* and *Gunsmoke*. Together we absorbed those idealized pictures of an American past and present and a glorious future. Beamed into white homes and Indian boarding schools alike, these shows taught us all about who mattered and who wasn't even there. Together we learned, right along with everyone else, that there are many ways we could disappear.

※　※　※

My father's brothers were sent to an Indian boarding school, and they brought the trauma home with them. They were sent to Pelican Lake Indian Residential School, which was located just outside Sioux Lookout in Northern Ontario and which operated from 1929 through 1969. My father once sent me a photograph taken of the

Pelican Lake Residential School hockey team. On the bottom right is my uncle Angus, a man who died before I was born. He looks like my youngest son.

Online archives at Algoma University include a photo album, and in that photo album are photographs of my uncles as young boys at the school. Years ago, my father and I went home to visit the reserve, and at a community dinner, we sat with an old friend of his named Kelly. Kelly had been a student at Pelican Lake with my uncles. My father asked me to look up the website on my phone and show Kelly this photo album. Kelly scrolled through the pictures, pointing out boys he remembered, laughing at some memories, and becoming suddenly silent at others. He remarked on who was still alive and who was not.

When Kelly got to a photograph of two young white women smiling at the camera, teachers at the school, he stopped scrolling. "That bitch," he said. Kelly pointed at one of the women, explaining to us that this young woman had sexually abused him. He told me what she had done to him, that he did not know how many others she had abused. We scrolled on and found some more photos of these two women photographed with boys. The women are smiling at the camera in these photographs too. I wonder about the expressions on the faces of the boys, the ones who aren't smiling, who are leaning slightly away.

Pelican Lake Residential School was built just outside Sioux Lookout, a small city four hours north of Thunder Bay, which is on the northern edge of Lake Superior. Much of the original building remains, alongside new construction. It is now called Pelican Falls First Nation High School and it is operated by the Northern Nishnawbe Educational Council. Although the residential school system has ended, many young people in the United States and Canada still need to leave their reservations to go to high school in cities. They stay in boarding homes and dormitories at places like Pelican Falls, youths as young as thirteen in cities for the first time, attending schools far from home.

My father and I visited the grounds of this school to which his brothers were taken. There is a memorial there, off to the side of the building, honoring the children who attended the school. Honoring those who never went home.

I walked to the train tracks and looked down the line to where it disappeared into the forest. I thought of something one of my cousins told me: that whenever railroad workers do repairs on these tracks, they find the bones of children who were trying to go home.

And how do we even begin to understand what it must have been like for these communities bereft of their children?

I participated in an exercise years ago meant to convey this. The facilitator asked for volunteers to play the various roles. Those representing the children in Indigenous communities were placed in the center of the room. They were surrounded by elders. The next circle out was the younger adults, then the older adults, and finally the leaders. She explained that it was the responsibility of the elders to teach and care for the smaller children and in turn the elders received care from the older children. We imagined the adults out tending to agriculture or hunting. The final volunteer needed was someone to play the role of the Indian agent, that government bureaucrat put in charge of the reserve. Because I hadn't wanted to participate, I was the only person left without a role. So it became my job to walk past the leaders, through the adults, and into the inner circle of elders.

Then I had to take the "children" by the hand and lead them out of the circles to the back of the room, where I had them face the wall. I was given a prop that represented the authority of the state—the capacity to use violence, if necessary, to ensure cooperation.

When I had the "children" take each other's hands and then took the hand of the first person, my eyes welled up with tears that I fought off for the rest of the exercise. The facilitator took us through the breakdown of the community as the various social roles began to unravel. When the children returned for visits, it was not as a group holding hands but as individuals who came intermittently. Children became teenagers who became young adults who often stopped coming home to these unraveled, unrecognizable communities, drifting into cities and towns. Disappearing.

Even as the government was taking their children, the tribes were experiencing other losses—disruptions they had been navigating for several generations. The loss of their children took place alongside the loss of land and relocations that we read about in chapter 3. It took place alongside the ravages of epidemics and military aggression.

Illness had raged across the continent, microbes rushing ahead of colonists on the goods that came to our communities through trading relationships. Illnesses like smallpox, tuberculosis, and measles killed up to 90 percent of some tribes. Remember that there was no wilderness for the settlers to inhabit—only depopulated spaces. In addition to the inadvertent spread of these illnesses, there is evidence of deliberate attempts at infecting Indigenous people. General Amherst recommended that blankets known to have been used by smallpox victims be distributed to Indians so that they would fall ill as well. His plan may not have been successful, but his willingness to try speaks loudly. Epidemics continued in waves through the nineteenth, twentieth, and twenty-first centuries, with consistently inadequate government response and disproportionate impact on Indigenous communities. There are, after all, many ways for people to disappear.

Military aggression took many forms. Two examples, separated by about thirty years, capture and in some ways bookend the ethnic cleansing of the West. Remember that earlier in the nineteenth century, the area west of the Mississippi was considered Indian Country. This was where the tribes had been relocated to, with the promise that they could live there in some freedom. But big brother was hungry, and the needs of an expanding empire threatened that precarious safety.

In 1862, Abraham Lincoln ordered the execution of thirty-nine Dakota men. The Dakota had been relocated several times and by this time were confined to part of southwest Minnesota, on land that was hard to live on and much smaller than the treaties previously agreed to. Food and trade goods that were supposed to come didn't, and the Dakota were starving. A local storeowner refused them credit for food and reportedly said, "Let them eat grass." Skirmishes between the Dakota and the settlers turned to war, and by the time it was over thirty-seven days later, many soldiers, settlers, and Dakota were dead. When the storeowner's body was found, his mouth was stuffed with grass.

Some of the Dakota fled, and others surrendered. Of the two thousand who were taken into custody, twenty were sentenced to prison, and 303 were sentenced to death, charged with rape, murder, and robbery. According to military practice at the time, all two thousand should have been released. Describing this in his book *Heartbeat of Wounded Knee*, David Treuer calls this the actions of a sovereign nation rising up against foreign invaders. It was a military action with a military result. But Lincoln ultimately approved thirty-nine executions in the largest mass hanging in US history. The rest of the surviving Dakota were evicted from the state of Minnesota and sent to reservations in Nebraska and the Dakotas.

Confederate soldiers, who also took up arms against the United States of America, were not hanged. In 1868, President Andrew Johnson granted them a pardon and an amnesty, restoring to them "all the rights, privileges, and immunities under the Constitution." Far from being shamed or exiled, many of the leaders of the former Confederacy were restored to positions of authority. Alexander Stephens, the vice president of the Confederacy, was elected to Congress and became the governor of Georgia. Robert E. Lee became the head of Washington College.

Following decades of genocide and ethnic cleansing, the Ghost Dance was spreading across multiple tribal groups. Beginning with the Lakota and spreading to others, the Ghost Dance was a message of hope that promised that the white invaders would leave and that everything would return to the way it had been. Native people began gathering in large numbers and dancing the Ghost Dance to see visions of those they had lost and to bring a new vision into being.

In his book *Our History Is the Future*, Lakota academic and activist Nick Estes describes the Ghost Dance as a "utopian dream that suspended the nightmare of the wretched present by folding the remembered experience of pre-colonial freedom into an anti-colonial future." Just as in the Anishinaabe flood narrative, the people were reaching back for their old ways in the hopes of creating something new. The Ghost Dance was less a religion than a shared vision of what was yet possible. A vision of a world without conquerors and invaders, a world without "white devils" who stole their children and killed their people.

And the US government saw it as a threat. Almost thirty years after the hanging of the Dakota, in December 1890, the US Cavalry opened fire on a camp of nearly three hundred Lakota ghost dancers near Wounded Knee Creek on the Pine Ridge Reservation of South Dakota. The fully armed US Cavalry came to one of these camps with a Hotchkiss gun, a cannon with a rotating barrel, and the intention of disarming the Lakota. One Lakota man refused to give up his rifle, and according to some witnesses, the rifle went off when he was grabbed by soldiers. The US Cavalry opened fire. At least 150 Lakota were killed and fifty wounded, including women and children. Because of a blizzard, it would be three days before the dead were buried. Twenty US soldiers were later awarded the Medal of Honor.*

Visiting Wounded Knee has become a kind of pilgrimage for Indigenous people. At some point, we all think about standing in those fields. We think about the ghosts that dance around us. Even if they aren't our ghosts, we know that they are relatives and that their losses are also ours. I went to Wounded Knee with my husband and middle son. In the Badlands of South Dakota, undulating grasslands drop off abruptly into distinctive rock formations. Sharp canyons and tall spires in red and gray layers dominate the landscape. At the Wounded Knee memorial, visitors tie tobacco ties—small scraps of cloth wrapped around pinches of tobacco—to the fencing. I added my own ties to those fluttering prayers, creating a visible presence of people who had disappeared.

---

* There is a push by Native leaders and some legislators to rescind these medals. Although about 900 Medals of Honor have been rescinded, most of these were related to the Civil War. As of November 2021, no medals related to Indian Wars have been rescinded. https://www.nytimes.com/2021/11/03/us/politics/rescind-medals-wounded-knee-massacre.html.

When we arrived at the memorial, storm clouds were gathering. A friend's cousin, Pte San Win, whose ancestors had been massacred at Wounded Knee, met with us. By the time she arrived, the wind made it impossible to talk, and we fled to our cars to wait it out. The wind eventually died down, and the sky cleared. When Pte San Win and I stood on top of a low rise, the world felt scrubbed clean. I looked down at the grasslands and thought about her relatives disappearing beneath the Hotchkiss gun, disappearing beneath the blizzard, disappearing into a mass grave.

There has always been resistance and refusal to disappear. Before Wounded Knee, there was the Battle of Little Big Horn, where General Custer and his unit were defeated by Lakota warriors. Our existence today is evidence of that refusal. But these policies had consequences, and over time, these disruptions and the losses of our land, of our relatives, and of our children piled one on top of the other. People can only take so much loss.

Our disappearance from these various landscapes isn't just something that happened, something tragic but unavoidable. It was deliberate. Disappearance was and is policy.

Indigenous people did not willingly disappear into reservations and boarding schools; the military and then the police were used to force compliance. There is a famous painting by Cree artist Kent Monkman called "The Scream," which depicts the moment that authorities come to a community to take children from parents and put them in residential schools. As with all Monkman's paintings, it is filled with movement and people. Officers of the Royal Canadian Mounted Police (RCMP), the federal police force in Canada, wearing red coats, and nuns and priests in their black robes are reaching for, pulling at, and carrying children away from mothers. The mothers reach out desperately to children already in the arms of priests; they wrap their arms protectively around others. In the foreground, an RCMP officer chases a small child, and in the background, three older children, maybe teenagers, run toward the woods.

Looking carefully at this image, I don't see fathers. I see men who are police officers and priests, I see women who are nuns and mothers. Where are the fathers of these children? There is one who may be a father, lying on the ground and barely visible, but it is unclear.

Fathers disappear.

In the United States, the military was tasked with clearing the West of Native people, with the help of local militias like the Texas Rangers. In Canada, that job fell to the Northwest Mounted Police, who eventually became the RCMP. These organizations—both military and paramilitary—took whatever actions they thought appropriate to protect and secure these new countries by enforcing the legislation and policies that would result in surrender or defeat. They fought us when they had to, contained us when they needed to, and disappeared us into reservations, jails, and residential schools.

For most people, a home means a father and mother, 2.3 children. The father protects and provides, the mother nurtures and cares, and the children grow up to do it all over again, as Pete Seeger sings, in houses "made of ticky tacky" where they all look "just the same." These are the family values that America is built on. But whose family is valued, and whose family is removed? Removals of all kinds mean that the homes of Black and Indigenous people, migrants, and those whose religious beliefs placed them outside of Christian norms are kept unstable and precarious.

Just as the Indian Removal Act of 1830 and the Dawes Act of 1887 were used to strip Native tribes of their land and force massive migrations that cleared the way for white land ownership, Reconstruction in the United States ensured that land remained in white hands. Immediately after the Civil War, some of the confiscated Confederate land was distributed to newly freed Black people, but those allocations were taken back as the government chose to reconcile with former Confederates instead of the formerly enslaved. Black people, even those who had small landholdings, were still forced to depend on white landowners for work.

Black families also migrated; they moved westward to Oklahoma, where the freedmen, formerly enslaved people who were tribal members, had land allotments and community. They moved north to cities like New York and Chicago, where they were safer but not safe. Slavery was abolished, but the beliefs that justified it were not. White supremacist attacks on the Black home persisted for decades after emancipation, regardless of where they lived. The race riots of Atlanta (1906), East St. Louis (1917), Omaha and Chicago (1919), and the massacre in Tulsa (1921) were coordinated attacks on Black prosperity. Black homes were confined to certain neighborhoods, and Indigenous homes were confined to reservations. Both types of home were precarious and impossible to protect.

❋   ❋   ❋

As boarding schools began to decline, another strategy of child removal was coming to the fore. Child protective services used the same language of safety that residential schools had used to separate Indigenous children from their families.

As a profession, social work, of which child welfare is one branch, emerged in the late nineteenth century as a way to manage the problem of poverty in a growing and prosperous country. Then as now, only middle- and upper-class women could afford to stay home. For the rest, both parents had to work long hours to earn enough money to pay for food and shelter. Industrial jobs were dangerous with high fatality rates, mortality rates in general were high for those living in poverty just as they are now, and then, just as now, many children lived in financially precarious single-parent households. Social workers initially focused on poverty, but by the 1920s, they were starting to focus more on families and children. The idea began to emerge that some children needed to be protected from their own families and placed with more suitable ones.

In the middle part of the century, as the horrors of the German concentration camps were made visible to the world, Canada and the United States began quietly redirecting the horror of residential schools to the more congenial removal of children from their families via the now fully engaged child welfare system. Instead of red-coated RCMP officers working with nuns and priests to tear children from their families, social workers, sometimes with police officers accompanying them, would take children from parents considered neglectful or dangerous and place them with other families. Once again, children were disappearing from reservations. But this time, instead of disappearing into schools, they were disappearing into white families.

Children were disappearing from the Indigenous communities that formed in cities too. The young people who earlier disappeared into Indian boarding schools often found it difficult to return to their reservations. They didn't speak the language, relationships had been severed, and there was little work. They drifted into cities, forming eddies and currents of relationship with other young people who were in similar circumstances, creating urban Indigenous communities out of multiple tribes. Cities had jobs, and government policies in the mid-twentieth century offered financial incentives to anyone willing to leave the reservation and move to the city. They had been promised a better life if they adopted the religion, rules, and language of the Americans. But they couldn't change the color of their skin, which affected the jobs they could get, the apartments they could rent, and the response of the police to their presence in some neighborhoods. This made it difficult for them to have the kind of homes that American society valued, and the impacts of relationships that were severed or institutionalized made it difficult to have the kind of families that US society valued.

Into these urban and reservation communities came child welfare workers, with clipboards full of assumptions about what good families look like. When we think of child safety, we generally think about physical abuse. But most referrals to child welfare agencies are based in these malleable, subjective, and culturally constructed ideas about "neglect" and "conflict." Neglect and family conflict happen in middle- and upper-middle-class families as well, but it is the neglect and conflict alleged in poor families that receive the most attention, that result in the removal of children.

Removal of Indigenous children from their families was so widespread that in Canada, it was given the name Sixties Scoop: the scooping of Indigenous children from their homes with little investigation before reaction. The Indigenous children scooped from their homes were adopted out to families as far away as Europe and New Zealand, echoing the earlier practice of putting children in residential schools far from home to discourage running away.

In the United States, the removal rates were so disproportionate that the Indian Child Welfare Act of 1978 was created to establish standards of placement and enable tribes to be involved in child welfare cases. Even so, the Sixties Scoop became the Millennium

Scoop, and in the United States and Canada, Indigenous children continue to be removed in disproportionate numbers. In May 2018, Dakota/Lakota writer Ruth Hopkins wrote a piece for *Teen Vogue* about the US foster care system and its failure to care for Native American children. She writes that by the 1970s, approximately 25–35 percent of Native children in the United States were placed in foster homes, adoptive homes, or institutional settings. Some 85 percent of those children were placed outside of their communities altogether. The 1978 Indian Child Welfare Act was supposed to address this disparity; thirty years later, however, serious disparities persist. American Indian children are almost twice as likely to be in foster care as white children; in South Dakota, they are eleven times more likely, making up 53 percent of the kids in care. Canadian numbers aren't any better: 7.7 percent of all children under the age of fifteen are Indigenous, but of all the children in foster care who are under fifteen, 52.2 percent are Indigenous.

I worked for a child welfare organization in Canada for sixteen years. I had not gone into social work with the intention of doing child welfare, but during a placement with a community organization, I discovered that I liked working with families. Working for an organization whose mandate was the protection of children seemed like a good place to do that. Like many of the people who had worked in boarding schools, I believed in my good intentions. I didn't think about the larger structure and the patterns that were at work.

There is no question: children deserve to be safe. But in all of my conversations at work about the risks that children faced inside their homes, we never talked about the risks that these children would face when we removed them. Most of the families that come into contact with child welfare services don't ultimately have their children removed from their care. That fear is ever present for parents, however, because its unspoken threat is behind every question, every suggestion or command. Parents know what the child welfare worker has the capacity to do.

For Black and Native families, who are already seen as potentially dangerous or unfit, the risks are even greater. I often see memes on social media about Native children who were unloved in residential schools growing up to be parents who struggle to love their children. While I understand that these messages are intended to elicit compassion, I worry about what it tells social workers about our parents and their capacity to love their children.

And what message does it send to a Black or Native child that their own Black or Native family was dangerous, and this white foster family is safe? Because Black and brown children, if they come into care, almost always wind up with white families. That's who usually makes it through the foster care approval process. I think often of the racially marginalized children I worked with during those years who would have wound up in white families without my intervention.

I worked with a child whose parents were Haitian refugee claimants and who had experienced significant trauma both in Haiti and after their refugee claim. I'll call the parents Lovely and Daniel and their son Junior. The story of this family's precarity goes back to the French colony of Haiti and its reliance on enslavement of Black people. It goes back to the Haitian Revolution of 1804, when these enslaved Africans revolted and freed themselves. It goes back to the French government imposing reparations—but not reparations paid to those who had formerly been enslaved. These reparations were levied *against* them. In other words, those who had been enslaved were forced to pay reparations to those who had enslaved them for the "theft" of their "property." These reparations were financed by French banks and the American Citibank. The amount, twenty-one billion in today's US dollars, was not paid off until 1947. This scheme is widely recognized as being responsible for Haiti's persistent poverty.

The story of this family's precarity rests in the wholly inadequate system that processes and supports migrants and refugees in Canada—not because of the people who do that work but because of the lack of government funding and commitment to caring for migrant people. Lovely and Daniel's housing and financial circumstances were precarious, and they were frequently homeless. This meant that accessing mental health services in any kind of meaningful way was impossible. We value homes, but we don't provide them. I think about the difference it would have made for Lovely and Daniel to have had stable housing and care for their physical and mental trauma, for them to be safe. But we save children and not families, so Junior was taken into foster care.

When Black and Indigenous children are placed in white foster homes, we don't think about what it tells them about who is safe and who is dangerous. For Junior, the only Black man he knew had been unpredictable and frightening. Children don't understand trauma and trauma responses, and although Daniel loved Junior deeply, he could also be volatile. One day, Junior was going to look into the mirror and see only Daniel. He needed to know that Black men are caring and compassionate, that they are good fathers who love their children.

While Junior was living in a white foster home, an opportunity came up for him to be adopted. This couple, we'll call them Evens and Madeline, was from Haiti and had relatives who still lived there. They made regular trips home to Haiti—and not to American-owned resorts where Haitians work in service jobs but to a community filled with friends and relatives. I worked hard at building my relationship

with Junior, driving him to visits with Evens and Madeline so that
he could build a relationship, so that he would have a family who
looked like him and, perhaps, in their love and care see the tender-
ness that trauma and an inadequate refugee system had stolen from
Daniel and Lovely. He would look in the mirror and know that they
had loved him too.

Junior's story has a happy ending. Evens and Madeline adopted
him, and as far as I know, they loved and cared for him in a stable
home. But he remains separated from his birth parents, who are con-
fused about what happened and where their son is. Their own precarious mental health and inability to remain in contact with child
welfare workers made it difficult, if not impossible, to know if they
understood what happened and why. So I don't know. Maybe it isn't
a happy ending.

Children deserve to be safe. But the language of safety has never
meant true safety for Indigenous children. Just as with Indian boarding schools, the vocabulary of "safe" and "educated" and "civilized"
has been used to justify war against our communities and to separate
us from our families. Policies that define what "acceptable" homes
and families look like disrupt our own family and communal practices. After governments and people with good intentions destabilize
our communities, the language of safety is used to destabilize them
further. If we wanted families to do well, we would put policies into
place that protect the family—that ensure they have homes and food
and all the things that our society says that people should have. But
we talk about children living in poverty, and children going hungry,
and children "at risk." We begin, with those words, the process of
disappearing them into white families.

When we got to the last room in our tour of the Woodland Institute, the guide gave us time for questions. Several people in the tour

group we had joined made comments about the good intentions of the teachers and the staff. Surely the people who operated and worked in these schools meant well? These teachers and custodians, these administrators and missionaries, these funders and government bureaucrats who paid the bills and kept the lights on. They just wanted to teach, to educate, to bring us civilization in the form of English and Jesus and little houses made of ticky-tacky. They wanted Indigenous children to be fed and safe from communities where there were poverty and danger.

They thought there was something wrong with us that they could fix. They didn't stop to think that there was something wrong with America or Canada that created these conditions. They never questioned why our communities were impoverished or dangerous. And they never wondered whether they, themselves, were the dangerous ones.

## Aambe

Poet Cheryl Savageau, of Abenaki descent, writes about the trouble she got into in graduate school when writing about the Indians who were rendered invisible in paintings and books. (You'll find lines from her poem at the beginning of this book.) "Stop writing what isn't in the text," her professor tells her. As you've seen, *not* being in the text is just our entire history.

At the end of chapter 1, you noticed our absence. Now think about that absence—in movies, books, conversations, and committees—and try insisting on our presence. Stop replacing us and begin the work of *re*-placing Black and Indigenous people into these landscapes.

That might mean stepping back from a committee to create space for Indigenous representation. It could mean suggesting a book written by an Indigenous author for your book club. It could mean speaking up and saying that yes, you can imagine such a thing happening.

Wherever you notice our absence, think about how you might be able to assert our presence.

# CHAPTER 5

# ERADICATION: THE VANISHED INDIAN

We disappeared from the landscape via military assaults and epidemics. We disappeared into boarding schools and then the child welfare system, which worked together to sever us from families and history, giving us nuclear families and a disjointed history in which we are repeatedly rescued by the very people who put us at risk. Sometimes we disappear into prison. And sometimes we just disappear.

People think of policing as eternal, as having always existed. But like child welfare and boarding schools, it evolved fairly recently to serve a particular purpose. When you move people off the land, they need to go somewhere, and people without land go to cities. Cities and villages have always had neighborhood watches and loosely organized citizen groups that managed antisocial behavior, but these were local and had limited power. In 1829, Robert Peel created London's Metropolitan Police Force to deal with the exploding urban population. This organization coordinated the various neighborhood watches, paid them, and in this way criminalized the poor for doing in public what the wealthy did in private. Peel had experience using the military in controlling the Irish people during the English colonization of Ireland, and he used the same strategies to control the urban poor. Strategies of containment and starvation were useful in clearing the American plains as well. After the West was won, the frontier was declared closed, and armies were replaced by police forces.

Prisons didn't always exist either. Somebody had to think them up, and eventually somebody did. Quakers thought that capital punishment, particularly as it existed in the late eighteenth century, was inhumane. So in 1790, they created prisons as a reform. Based on the Calvinist idea that solitude and silence could lead to repentance—to penitence for wrongdoing—the Quakers created "penitentiaries" as a place for that solitude. Many traditions, Indigenous ones included, contain elements of solitude: time apart in fasting and prayer to realign relationship to self and environment. But chosen solitude is much different from forced isolation. Solitary confinement is now recognized by many as tortuous in its own right, but at the time, it was conceived of as a reform.

Between 2012 and 2019, Adam Capay, a twenty-six-year-old man from my reserve, Lac Seul First Nation, spent 1,647 days in solitary confinement while awaiting trial in Thunder Bay, Ontario. The UN Mandela Rules say that prisoners shouldn't be alone for more than fifteen consecutive days. Adam was alone for more than one hundred times that. His story is one of tragedy and aggression, and he is both victim and perpetrator. For 1,647 days, he was alone, spending months in Plexiglas cells, with lights on twenty-four hours a day. His time in solitude was devastating for his mental health. Perhaps unsurprisingly, he offended again shortly after he was released. It did not lead to realignment or repentance.

In 1790, the Walnut Street Jail in Philadelphia, Pennsylvania, was the first institution in the United States built to punish and rehabilitate prisoners. It had sixteen solitary cells. Before long, the

Eastern Pennsylvania Penitentiary, the first prison to be fully built using the theory of solitary confinement, was designed and operated by Quakers. Women's prisons, another reform that became necessary because housing women with men was dangerous, came later in the nineteenth century. With this new space to incarcerate women, increasing numbers of women went to prison.

Before the Civil War, Black people were owned and controlled, whether they labored in fields or houses and whether they lived on plantations or in cities. After the Civil War, they were legally freed but still controlled. The Thirteenth Amendment abolished slavery and involuntary servitude *except* as a punishment for crime. From their inception, prisons have been expected to pay their own way, and leasing convicts has been a constant source of revenue. After the Civil War, large numbers of newly freed Black people were leaving plantations for cities or seeking their own land upon which to farm and build. It is no coincidence that with the powerful as hungry for land as the leaders of empire in the United States are, the demographics of the prison population changed dramatically. It was no longer poor whites who needed to be controlled and excluded; Black people were moved from the land and into prison yards.

In *We Do This 'Til We Free Us*, prison abolitionist Mariame Kaba writes that the prison system saw a "massive population surge [in] the 1980s, when de-industrialization created the need for dungeon economies to replace lost jobs, and a backlash against the Civil Rights Movement and other social gains by Black people propelled heightened efforts at social control." Civil rights are precarious victories, and every backlash is clothed in the language of safety. Settler colonialism sweeps Black people into prisons, where they work off their room and board in fields and poultry plants, manufacturing and textiles.

Allotment took place about twenty years after the Civil War, moving Indians off the land so coveted by hungry settlers. We, too, moved into cities and then prisons, disappearing at rates disproportionate to our population. In the United States, the rate of imprisonment for Native Americans is double that of white Americans, and in states with large Native populations, that rate can be as high as seven times. For every one hundred thousand people in each racial category, there are 1,291 who are Native, 2,306 who are Black, and 450 who are white in prison. In Canada, we make up about 5 percent of the population but account for almost 30 percent of federal inmates. Indigenous women account for almost 42 percent of the incarcerated. There is either something very wrong with us, or there is something very wrong with the system itself. And there is nothing wrong with us.

Much crime is related to vagrancy, which is vague and useful for controlling excess populations. Vagrancy laws emerged in the Middle Ages to control peasants who were no longer tied to particular lords. These laws made it a crime for a person to wander about without any visible means of support, effectively making it illegal to be homeless and without a job. These laws are expressed in a number of ways, ranging from loitering charges to carding. Carding, or street checks, is a practice used by police officers to check the identity of somebody who is not doing anything obviously wrong but who is occupying a place the police believe they have no reason to be. In practice, that has meant stopping racially marginalized men who are in predominantly white neighborhoods and documenting their names. Over time, they become "known to police," suggesting something shady and questionable.

Slave codes empowered citizens to perform these checks on Black people, questioning their right to be anywhere. In Canada from 1885 to 1951, there was a pass system, which controlled when and under what circumstances adult Indians could leave the reserve and that made them subject to questioning by police and citizens. Although slave codes and the pass system have been long abolished, neighborhood watches serve a similar purpose. When George Zimmerman murdered Trayvon Martin and when Gerald Stanley murdered Colten Boushie, these underlying beliefs about who belongs where and who has the right to question or protect ensured their acquittals.

In addition to criminalizing homelessness, vagrancy laws are also used to criminalize prostitution, public drunkenness, gambling, and criminal association. The criminalizing of sex work forces many of those already on the margins further from safety and into increasingly dangerous and precarious circumstances. Probation and parole orders usually include stipulations against avoiding criminal association, something that is difficult to do when you are part of a population that is as deeply criminalized as Black and Indigenous communities. It makes it hard to find the kind of work that is deemed acceptable. It is difficult to find or afford housing, creating a vicious cycle that is difficult to break. With the influx of Native people into urban settings, community centers emerged to provide a wide range of programs and social activities. The Friendship Center I attend created a men's only night so that men could participate in programming without violating their release conditions by being in the same building as women or children. These rules that are couched in the language of safety make participating in the things that make us human very difficult. And so we disappear into prisons.

And sometimes Indigenous people simply disappear.

The story of Pocahontas is familiar, but the familiar story couldn't be farther from the truth. It is told as a love story when it is actually the story of an abduction. She is, perhaps, our first Missing Sister.

Her name was Metoaka—Pocahontas was a nickname—and she was the daughter of a Wampanoag chief. Metoaka was twelve when she met John Smith, and she may indeed have saved his life. But it was John Rolfe she eventually married, years after she had been kidnapped by the English and held by them for a year. Recounting this story in *The Baptism of Early Virginia*, historian Rebecca Anne Goetz writes that, at the time of her kidnapping, Metoaka was married to one of her own people. The sea captain who kidnapped her demanded a ransom, which her father did not pay. (Perhaps he did not "negotiate with terrorists.") After more than a year of captivity, Metoaka converted to Christianity and took the name Rebecca. She agreed to marry Rolfe, and they moved to London, where she is buried.

We don't know why Metoaka made the choices that she did. But we know that it began with an abduction. We also know that women who marry into patriarchal societies tend to become what David W. Anthony calls "hyper-correct imitators." They become more proper than the ones who were born within the society, in order to keep themselves safe, to feel less vulnerable. They do what they can to feel safe. And they still aren't safe.

Just as we have all been touched by prisons and boarding schools, we have all been touched by violence against and disappearance of our women. The rate of violence against Indigenous women and girls and two-spirit people is heartbreaking. (The term *two-spirit* is a translation of the Anishinaabe word niizh manidoowag. *Two-spirit* emerged as a way to reclaim acceptance of people who do not fit neatly into a male-female binary and who are not exclusively attracted to what is thought of as the opposite gender. As with any broad term, like our earlier discussion of the terms for Native people, it doesn't capture the diversity of attitudes regarding gender and sexuality in Native American tribes. Yet it is useful as shorthand, so I'll use it here.)

Think about the way that patriarchy devalues women in general and Black and Indigenous women in particular. Think about the way that it ostracizes and demonizes queer people. The homicide rate for Native women is almost six times as high as the rate for non-Native women, and while most women tend to be killed by somebody within their racial group, this is not true for Native women. We are more likely to be in relationships with white men. We are more likely to be exploited sexually by white men. And we are more likely to be killed or assaulted by white men.

In her book *The Beginning and End of Rape*, Mvskoke author and academic Sarah Deer notes how incomplete numbers about gendered violence are because the information simply isn't reported, recorded, or reliably investigated. In Canada from the 1990s to the early 2000s, serial killer Robert Pickton murdered forty-nine women, mostly Native, whose disappearances were not taken seriously by police because they were sex workers from East Vancouver. He was eventually charged and convicted. But police forces do not appear to have learned from this mistake, because across the United States and Canada, Native women continue to go missing, and their disappearances continue to be dismissed.

In the fall of 2021, Gabby Petito's disappearance dominated the news cycle. *Seattle Times* columnist Naomi Ishisaka noted that her case joined those of Laci Peterson and Natalee Holloway, white women whose disappearances resulted in vast, sympathetic publicity. This public attention is denied to disappeared Black and Indigenous women. She quotes journalist Maria Schiavocampo, who said, "This actually has real life implications for women of color. Why? This makes them less safe because perpetrators, predators, know that if you want to get away with murder, you seek the victim that no one is going to look for."

Until very recently, neither the FBI nor the RCMP kept records that identified missing women by race, and often the reports of missing Indigenous women were not taken seriously. Authorities often disregarded the missing as being sex workers or women on a binge. Families heard, "She'll come home when she's sober," and so the numbers of those who are *officially* missing are low.

But we know. The families know. We also know the first forty-eight hours of a missing-person investigation are critical. After that time period, the trail goes cold and just gets colder, and we were getting left out in the cold.

So in response to this inadequate reporting, recording, and investigating, a movement began. An initial hastag, #MMIW, expanded to #MMIWG and then to #MMIWG2S* so that people could begin to share and crowdsource information on who has gone missing. Native women began creating databases and maps drawn from information provided by the friends and family members of the missing. Annual marches and vigils began in East Vancouver and spread across Canada, often held on the steps of police stations with signs bearing the names of women missing but not investigated. These women forced the ones who are supposed to be protecting us to do their job. To notice the epidemic of MMIWG2S.

And although former Prime Minister Stephen Harper declined to investigate this "sociological phenomenon" and insisted that these

---

* "MMIW" stands for "missing and murdered Indigenous women," "MMIWG": "missing and murdered Indigenous women and girls," and "MMIWG2S": "missing and murdered Indigenous women and girls and two-spirit people."

cases be seen as individual crimes, this direct action eventually forced the Canadian government to hold a National Inquiry into Missing and Murdered Indigenous Women and Girls. Their report, *Reclaiming Power and Place*, was released in June 2019 after two years of hearings and testimony. It contains the testimony of thousands of family members and survivors, 231 calls for justice, and named this "sociological phenomenon" *genocide*.

Canada's report on MMIWG2S is the first time that an official body has used the term *genocide* in relation to the actions of Canada or the United States. The Truth and Reconciliation Report about the residential school system in Canada, published a few years earlier, stopped short of this definition, calling it a "cultural genocide," which is not a legal term. The commissioners of Canada's report on MMIWG2S knew that their decision to use this word would be controversial, and so they included a supplementary report laying out the legal basis. Canadian news outlets tripped over each other, writing outraged editorials about how it wasn't an actual genocide. Genocide lite, maybe? The report deals specifically with Canada, but so many of the policies, actions, or inactions are devastatingly similar in the United States.

The sterilization of Native women in the United States and Canada goes back to the early twentieth century, when concerns about population control combined with eugenics. Policies began to target women who were seen to be defective: generally those who were Black, Indigenous, chronically poor, or deemed mentally unfit. Given how frequently it is Black and Indigenous women who are also chronically poor or deemed mentally unfit, this, too, amounts to genocide. Laws that permitted sterilization without consent remained on the books until the 1970s.

In Canada, a class-action lawsuit alleges that this practice continued until 2018. In the fall of 2020, a whistleblower alleged that migrant women, many of whom are indigenous to Central America, were being sterilized without their knowledge or consent in an ICE detention center in Georgia. In her book *Reproductive Justice*, white academic and activist Barbara Gurr describes the legal and social history of this, as well as contemporary medical practices and funding structures that effectively continue this practice. She notes that "between 1968 and 1982, 42 percent of Native women of childbearing age were sterilized compared with 15 percent of white women." On some reserves, up to 80 percent of women were sterilized. Gurr is not suggesting that all of these sterilizations were coerced. But as with all disparities, we need to think about *why* it exists. What options are, or are not, made available?

When I still worked in child welfare, I attended a training about case management of people with fetal alcohol spectrum disorder, a brain injury caused by the use of teratogenic drugs like alcohol during pregnancy. The trainer spoke about giving her clients their monthly funding *after* proof of a birth control injection. She felt it was kinder than taking their children, and a room full of social workers agreed with her. Wouldn't it be kinder to create supports that would help them parent?

※　※　※

I attended a vigil for the missing and murdered in Toronto several years ago. One of the speakers was a woman who recounted her experience with the Toronto Police Services, which not only refused to acknowledge her account of being sexually assaulted but placed her in custody for being disorderly. They also refused to acknowledge her gender identity and placed her in a unit with men—where she was sexually assaulted again.

Standing there with others, I remembered a time I came close to being a name on a sign instead of being a person who holds a sign. I came so close. When I was in high school, I went to a dance, and at that dance, I met a cute boy. It was common then, as now, for groups of high school kids to rent motel rooms in which to hang out afterward. So we went back to his group's room. My friends came into the room a little while later and said that we had to go. It was late, they said; we had to go. Now. I was annoyed, but my friends were my ride, so we left together.

Later, they told me that they had overheard the cute boy's friends talking about a girl who was in their room. About how they were going to go back to the room and leave that girl in a ditch when they were done with her.

My friends realized they were talking about me.

Did those high school boys know I was Native? I went to a high school that was mostly Italian, and people often assumed that I was also Italian. I took pleasure in correcting them, so it may have come up. Or it may not have, and I don't know. But that's the problem. When these things happen—and they happen disproportionately to Native people—we sometimes don't know. Was it just because I'm a woman? Was it because I am Native? Was it both?

*When* these things happen.

Years later, I volunteered at an Aboriginal AIDS/HIV conference. I offered to help with the registration desk because the work would introduce me to people. I had just reconnected with my father, and I was looking for ways to build connection with Indigenous communities I did not know and who turned out to be all around me. During lulls in the conference schedule, those of us who were working registration would talk about our lives, what brought us here, where home was. At one point, a young man working the registration desk with me commented that when he gets beaten up, he never knows if it's because he's Blackfoot or because he's gay. Maybe it's both, he said.

*When* he gets beaten up.

Before I studied social work, I worked for a sexual assault center. In the United States and Canada, victims of sexual assault are seen by a specially trained nurse, often in a separate suite of rooms where they receive medical care and can speak with police if they wish. My role was to go to the hospital and provide support while the medical treatment and collection of evidence was completed.

One weekend, the police brought in a young white woman who was intoxicated. Officers explained that they had found her wandering a downtown street, and since she looked disheveled, they wanted to be sure she was okay. She insisted that she had not been assaulted, that she had been out drinking with friends who ditched her and she wanted to go home. The police officers left, and we continued to speak with her about the evening. She maintained that there had been no sex, consensual or otherwise, and she wanted to go home. We gave her information on sexual assault and called her a cab.

A few days later, another young woman, who was Native, called the center wanting to talk to a counselor. She had been sexually assaulted after a night of drinking, and when police found her, they picked her up for being drunk and disorderly and held her in custody overnight. She had been distraught when they found her, disheveled and crying, and they must have attributed this to her intoxication. When she was released the following day, she went home. By the time she contacted the center about the assault, several days had passed. I don't know why she didn't call the 24/7 crisis line, but I do know that sometimes when we experience a trauma, we focus on our immediate need for safety and comfort, and that's what she did. She showered and bathed and washed her clothes. Any evidence that might have been collected was long gone. We provided her with counseling and support, which was all she was asking for. She was not interested in reporting the assault to the police.

What accounted for these two very different experiences? Was it just different police officers with different experiences? Or was it because the first young woman was white, and the second was Native? Did the police see a Native woman and assume that she was just drunk and sexually available anyway? We are all haunted by this question: When we are assaulted, is it just because we are in the wrong place at the wrong time? Is it because we are Native? Both?

*When* we are assaulted.

The Canadian Inquiry into Missing and Murdered Indigenous Women and Girls found that police do not take concerns about assaults and sexual assaults of Native women seriously. Testimony after testimony was presented to the commission, stories about how the police disregarded their concerns or refused to investigate. The report documents a history of this disregard going back to the early years of Canada's colonial history. Willie James Jennings writes about this in *The Christian Imagination*, noting how early missionaries saw and described the Native women as sexually promiscuous and blamed them for the sexual sins of the men. Scholars Sarah Deer and Rebecca Anne Goetz remark on it in their histories. It's inescapable because it is right in their own journals and diaries: the way that they saw us, thought about us, blamed us.

Sexual assault is often framed in terms of what the victim was wearing or doing or drinking. But sexual assault is the imposition of power; it is about who the victim *is*. And that is something that Black and Native women and girls and queer or two-spirit people can't do anything about. White women are taught that they can keep themselves safe as long as they conform to certain ideas about how proper white women behave. It isn't true, but it provides them with the illusion of control; it is a way of showing the world that they are respectable and worthy of care, not like "those other women" who are not worthy, who are "asking for it." Black and Native women, as well as queer and two-spirit people (who exist outside of certain ideas about what men and women are supposed to be like), were seen in the past, and still today, as always sexually available, always promiscuous, always outside of good moral existence.

We can try to conform to these ideas of how proper women behave, but it doesn't keep us safe. Because we, like the land, are rapable. Sarah Deer writes, "Rape embodies the worst traits of colonization in its attack on the human body, disrespect for physical boundaries, and disregard for humanity." This echoes a warning from Leviticus 19:29, "Do not degrade your daughter by making her a prostitute, or the land will turn to prostitution and be filled with wickedness." The way we treat children, our own or the children of others, is the way we treat the land. The way we treat the land is the way we treat our children.

Sexual violence is not just something that happens to women. Our men also experience extraordinary rates of sexual violence, both in the way that they are seen as predators who are guilty before they've done anything at all as well as the sexual assaults that are endemic to prisons, or "rape factories," as I have heard them described. We recognize that the prison rape of women is a problem, but when men go to prison, rape is either a joke or a threat. Sexual violence and threats of sexual violence are used by police to gain compliance. The assaults on our boys and young men moved from residential schools, to foster care, to prison.

There are many ways for us to disappear.

❋    ❋    ❋

Bella is the daughter of Thelma and Harry. She was born in British Columbia, where she and her stuffed lamb entered the foster care system. Thelma is Salish, part of a group of tribes that live in the watershed where British Columbia and Washington State meet the Pacific Ocean. Thelma is the daughter of Jesse and Mary Ann. Jesse and Mary Ann attended St. Mary's Indian Residential School in Mission, British Columbia. It was common to separate family members, and so while they went to St. Mary's, their relatives attended the Kamloops Indian Residential School. There, on a summer day in 2021, the unmarked graves of 215 children were revealed.

My friend Sarah obtained guardianship of Bella and her little stuffed lamb. We saw each other recently at a vigil for those children at the Kamloops Indian School. She told me that Bella's grandparents had relatives who attended that school. That she has relatives in those graves.

I saw her a few months later at a Sisters in Spirit vigil. Sarah's family organizes the local event because her cousin, a white woman, went missing in an area of British Columbia where a number of Native women have also gone missing, and the police have not been helpful. We gather together to demand justice for all of our missing sisters and brothers, thinking about aunties and uncles, cousins and parents, and our own close calls.

Over the course of the summer of 2021, hundreds of unmarked graves would be revealed across Canada. In the United States, Secretary of the Interior Deb Haaland announced the Federal Indian Boarding School Initiative to investigate these schools. In November 2021, researchers announced that they found the names of 102 Native American students who died at the Genoa Indian School, which operated from 1884 to 1934 in Genoa, Nebraska. They said that the true death toll is probably higher.

Across the United States and Canada, people are looking for the graves of children who, like our missing women, were known to us but not documented. Graves and losses documented in reports that nobody reads. Vigils held on the steps of the authorities who promised, and failed, to protect us.

Nii'kinaaganaa.

## Aambe

Orange Shirt Day was started by Phyllis Webstad, whose orange shirt was taken from her on the day she started at the St. Joseph Mission Residential School. In Canada, Orange Shirt Day is now a national holiday: the national day for truth and reconciliation. People wear orange shirts to honor residential school survivors, and many of the shirts are emblazoned with the words "every child matters."

It is important, when we mark significant days like this, to think about what we are doing. Days and vigils—those meant to honor those who attended residential schools or who disappeared into prisons or who simply disappeared—mean different things in different communities. For Indigenous people, these are moments to collectively grieve. For others, they may mean something different.

Take some time to reflect on why these days and vigils are necessary. Think about what our countries and churches have done, are doing. If you hear of a vigil or rally taking place in your area, attend it. Listen to the speakers. Introduce yourself to somebody.

# FLOOD

Grief is the persistence of love. It sees my ancestors in stalks of corn and hears them whisper when I pour wild rice through my hands. It fills my bag with nettles and reminds me to be gentle when I strip bark from larch or dogwood.

Grief is the sound of thunder you feel deep in your chest, the lingering smell of sage hours after it is burnt.

Grief is the forgetting of names. It does not know which place the ancestors' feet last touched before leaving home forever. It looks back over shoulders and sees only darkness. Stolen lives means stolen history means no thread to pick up and follow home.

Grief holds the accumulation of centuries in its hands and watches it turn to ash and then reaches out for more. Grief is consuming and consumed, an endless cycle of loss.

We take a moment and pause. So much loss, so many missed opportunities for relationship and community. How can we not be overwhelmed by it? These histories, these memories: they come in like the tide. Each wave pushes the ocean further inland until we are submerged.

In the harbor of a nearby town, there is a hurricane protection barrier. It is a wall with a gate that protects the town from hurricanes. But as the seas continue to rise and the hurricanes become more intense, the townspeople behind this wall of rock and steel know that it won't protect them forever.

We are like this. We hold grief at bay with walls of rock and steel, fearing the time when they fail to protect us. We fear the ocean, the weight of this history we cannot change. We fear the rip tides of systems we feel helpless to change. Imagining possibility seems so far away. What if we can't swim?

But.

What if we can?

It was dark. And wet. Nanaboozhoo found himself floating in the water. He pulled himself up onto a log and called out to the other animals, who were paddling about nearby or flying overhead. The sun came up, and it was water as far as he could see. There had been a flood, and it had caught all of creation by surprise.

When the world was originally created, there was balance, and all the different parts of creation lived in good relationship with each other. They met their obligations, took care of each other. But over time, humans grew selfish and began fighting with each other, first one against the other and then as groups against other groups. The Creator, and perhaps the world herself, waited to see if we would remember ourselves. But we didn't, and our actions put all of creation at risk. So there was a flood.

And that's how Nanaboozhoo found himself on a log with the animals. He remembered the earlier story: how the first woman had fallen from skyworld and had used some mud to create this world, in that way becoming the mother of everything. So he told the animals his plan to swim down through the water to collect some mud so that the winds could blow and create, re-create, the world.

Nanaboozhoo held his breath and swam down as far as he could, but he came up gasping. He told the creatures that he could not hold his breath that long or swim that far.

Other animals tried. Loon said she could do it because she dives for food. Otter and Mink tried their skills in swimming and diving. Even Turtle, who hibernates in shallow mud and knows how to swim, tried. But the water was deep, and none of them was able to hold their breath that long or swim that far.

Then Muskrat said he would do it.

Muskrats are small animals, only about two to four pounds and about two to three feet tip to tail. They are comfortable in the water and strong swimmers. They can hold their breath for long periods. The other animals scoffed, but Nanaboozhoo quieted them and encouraged Muskrat to try.

Muskrat was gone for a long time. Bubbles surfaced. Muskrat surfaced. Nanaboozhoo took his small form into his hand and realized that he was no longer breathing. He turned to the other creatures and told them, sadly, that Muskrat had drowned.

Then he noticed Muskrat's clenched paw. There, in his paw, was some mud. Nanaboozhoo took that mud and put it on the log. He drummed and sang, and the animals danced, and the four winds blew, and the mud became land that spread out far and wide.

And the world was made new.

Floods are destructive, and grief is part of our great flood stories: grief for what is lost, grief because there is much that can never be restored, and grief because even what is restored will always be tinged with that loss. Many ancestors were overcome by the waters, and many lives were ended before they had the opportunity to become ancestors.

In the first part of this book, we examined those losses and the corrosive, corrupting nature of settler colonialism. Colonization did wash over the Western Hemisphere like a flood, engulfing and overwhelming it. Like Muskrat, we dove through those waters, looking for something with which we could rebuild.

But the flood metaphor is limited, as all metaphors are. We have surfaced, alive—out of breath, perhaps, but still breathing. And the harms of colonization are not something that just happened; they are not acts of nature or even divine judgment. Despite what many people are desperate to believe, they are not the unintended consequences of misguided but otherwise good intentions.

And so now we build. With everything we learn, we add to our handful of mud. We have noticed and acknowledged. We have considered promises and places. We have begun to think about challenging the things that we hear and about how to begin *re*-placing those who are not seen. And now we turn to the process of rebuilding. We turn to the work of becoming kin to the land and each other, understanding our responsibilities. Because for Indigenous peoples, kinship means responsibilities.

Just as Muskrat picked up that handful of mud, we are, in the words of the Seventh Fire, picking up our bundles. They will help us to restore what was lost and, hopefully, guide us to a path that is lush and green, a new world.

We pick up our own bundles, not those that belong to somebody else. The knowledge that other bundles contain can illuminate and inform. But we need to be sure that what we are picking up is our own.

Biskaabiiyang.

Now we will begin to return to ourselves.

# CHAPTER 6

# THE LAND: OUR ANCESTOR

We begin with stones. In the Anishinaabe universe, even before the thoughts of Kiche Manidou—the Creator, or Great Mystery—there was what Louise Erdrich calls "a conversation between stones."

When I was in grade 9, my science teacher asked the class if stones were alive. We were learning the seven criteria of life. After reviewing the list, we said that no, stones were not alive. He asked us if we were sure. And so we went over the criteria again and told him yes, we were sure. He said that it might be that stones did things more slowly than we could measure. Could it be that we lacked the ability to see these things in stones? Or could the criteria be wrong? Then he smiled.

I don't think my teacher was suggesting that stones are alive; I think he wanted us to remember that science is the asking of questions and the constant adjustment of what we think we know. Later, in physics, we would learn about how some matter exists as both wave and particle, depending on how you look at it. Perspective matters.

This possibility—of something like a stone being alive—has stayed with me. Ojibwe Anishinaabe author and academic Lawrence Gross would agree with this science teacher. In his book

*Anishinaabe Ways of Knowing and Being*, he writes about the Anishinaabe language being more suited for quantum physics than English because it understands the dynamic nature of creation, particle and wave. It is a verb-based language, which talks about what things do rather than what they are. We are not human beings; we are *humans being*.

For the Anishinaabeg, stones may be alive. Our word for stone is *asin*. And it is animate. English is a highly adaptive and creolizing language, but it organizes the world into discrete subjects and then describes what those subjects are. So we shouldn't be surprised that our whole society is atomized into separate things. Grammar often divides things into male and female, most obviously in languages like French and Italian, but English, too, is concerned with gender.

Anishinaabemowin, as well as many other languages, is concerned with the action and relationship—whether things are animate or inanimate. That is revealed by the kinds of verbs that are used to describe what is happening. In English, I would say that the man "hit" his dog or that rain "hit" the ground. Same verb. In Anishinaabemowin, we would use different verbs depending on whether or not the thing being hit is animate.

But even being inanimate does not preclude something from having spirit. In his discussion about grammar in Anishinaabemowin, Gross tells an entertaining story about his moccasins (which are inanimate) being able to hit him because inanimate things can still act on animate things. His moccasins can't hit his socks, though, because his socks are also inanimate. How unfair, he says, even if it is grammatically correct.

It is not only the Anishinaabe for whom stones might be alive. The Indigenous people of Australia understand stones to have deep knowledge, holding memory and having spirit. Tyson Yunkaporta, an

Australian writer and carver and member of the Apalech clan, writes about the sentience of rocks in his book *Sand Talk*. He says you can't just pick one up and take it home, because you disturb its spirit, and it will disturb you. There is a shed full of them at Uluru, the massive sandstone monolith formerly known as Ayers Rock, that holds the stones that tourists have sent back. Despite having been told not to take rocks home, some people do, and then many report having bad dreams and bad luck. Some send them back.

I think about my own collection of stones—stones that I have picked up from various vacations and brought home. It's been a while since I've done that. I didn't have any kind of epiphany nor any bad dreams or bad luck. One day, I simply stopped doing it. I can't even say it was a conscious decision. Sometimes we learn to listen to things without realizing it.

The Sámi, an Indigenous people who live in Northern Europe, also talk about living stones. In her book *The Hebrew Bible and Environmental Ethics*, Norwegian Hebrew Bible scholar Mari Joerstad introduces us to a text that is filled with other-than-human persons, alive in the way that Gross and Yunkaporta describe and which is somehow missing from churches. She invites us to consider the world that the ancient Hebrew writers lived in as a "world [that] contained sentient, spiritual beings."

This world sounds more like what I hear from Anishinaabe authors and elders than anything I hear in church. Joerstad draws together these things: the sense of the ancient Hebrew with the Indigenous people living in Norway. She writes about Sámi reindeer herder and philosopher Nils Oskal describing the relationship that the Sámi have with *siedi* stones, to which they give gifts of coins or tobacco. Outsiders often mistake this courtesy—this recognition of life and connection—for worship. But it is part of a way of understanding our place in the world: we are in the midst of sentient beings with whom we are in relationship, whether we acknowledge it or not.

Are the stones alive? Can rocks cry out?

I want us to consider our relationship with land—to think about it beyond squabbling over ownership and rights and to think about responsibilities and reciprocal relationship. To think of ourselves as a part of creation rather than apart from it. What if the land is a being in its own right? That concept is not as foreign as you might think. And what if the land and all that grows from it and on it and in it are sentient beings in their own right? Then we need to make material changes that restore the land to our original agreements. We need to remember that the land belongs to itself, and everyone belongs to the Creator.

Land is our first relationship, and it is the first relationship that we need to restore. We are used to standing on it, planting in it, and marveling at it, but our relationship with it is complicated and colonial. We buy and sell it, extract resources from much of it, and then idealize parts of it.

We can't always go home. The reality is that because of fractured relationships, displacement, forced and unforced migrations, we may not know where home is. My friends who are part of the Black diaspora have talked about the heartbreak of not knowing the places their ancestors called home. Colonialism has disconnected us from land, severed us from that first relationship, often through violence. We need to restore our relationship with the land around us. That means going outside, as my son is prone to remind me. It means noticing and listening.

The first thing that Nanaboozhoo did was name things as he walked through the land. Naming creates relationships, reveals identity. Think about the way that you named children or pets, the care you took to think about who they were and your hopes for them. Perhaps the name represented other family members, significant places or events, or persistent behavior. Names are rarely given without thought to the one being named and the relationship that exists.

Governments are increasingly restoring Indigenous names to parks and streets, reminding people that these places had an existence before Europeans arrived. In 2015, the US Department of the Interior officially changed the name of Mount McKinley back to Denali, which is what the local Koyukon people had called it for centuries.

So we name the land, claiming relationship to it. And what if the land also claims us?

※　※　※

I reconnected with my father when I was in my late twenties, and shortly after that, he took me home to Sioux Lookout. It was the first time I had been home since leaving as a toddler, and I did not know what to expect. Going home is fraught with hopes and unrealistic expectations, and I had plenty of both and a lot of hours to ruminate on them.

It's a long drive from Niagara Falls to Sioux Lookout; people don't often realize how massive the province of Ontario is. You can start in Ontario, drive for twenty-four hours, and still be in Ontario. The geography changes, and although the highway goes up and down as it travels around Lake Superior, you are mostly going up into the Canadian Shield. There are long stretches empty of people, towns that you blink and miss—and then we were there. But not really there.

When I went home for the first time, there was no road into the reserve, so we stayed at a cabin nearby. My father pointed across the lake to Frenchman's Head and told me that's where the reserve is. Although there is a road now, in the mid-1990s, the people who lived there got in and out of the community by boat. There are still many reserves scattered throughout northern Canada that are accessible only by boat or plane, ice roads in the winter.

My father took me to Umfreville, a nearby community that had grown up around a lumber mill. That town is one of the ones where my mother had taught, and it is where my father and his family lived. Nobody had lived there for years when we visited it. There are fields of tall grass with a few wooden structures. He pointed at various buildings, telling me what they used to be. Some cousins happened to be in Umfreville that day, although I don't remember why they were there. Perhaps they were berry-picking, because there are a lot of blueberry bushes in northern Ontario. I took out the photo album I brought with me. It held photographs of me as a baby, pictures of my father and uncles, my grandmother, other children. They looked at the pictures and remembered stories, talked about who was still alive and who wasn't. Remembering what they used to be.

On that visit, I met my grandmother, living by then in Sioux Lookout, and it was a bittersweet meeting. All these moments were fraught with hope and unrealistic expectations because, like Umfreville itself, we are not what we used to be. Our lives have moved in different directions, and our shared memories stop at the same place as the photographs that recorded them. There were people who remembered me, people who remembered stories about me, and in the intervening years, they had periodically wondered what had happened to me. This was not a surprise. I had also leafed through the photo album and wondered what had happened to them.

But what was a surprise was the undeniable sensation that the land and water remembered me too. I stood beneath stands of black spruce and looked across the lake, and it felt so familiar that it ached. I went down to the rocky beach and put my hands in the water, and it remembered me. I cannot tell you how or why I knew that. It was completely unexpected, this sensation of both remembering and being remembered. I can only describe it as electric.

Since that time, I have had other fleeting reminders that the land is alive in ways I am only beginning to understand. I told you that I had stopped collecting stones, and that is mostly true. But this past summer when I went home again, we camped at provincial parks around Lake Superior. At one of them, my husband brought me a stone he had picked up on a beach covered in round stones. When I held it in my hand, it felt like mine. Not mine like a thing that was now in my possession but mine like my children are mine and like my parents are mine. We belonged to each other.

And I thought about the roundness of this granite, the smoothness of it, and the amount of time that must have taken. How patient the stone and the water were. The length of that relationship. Stones are ancient, older than water, older than time. Bones of the earth. They've been through so many worlds, so many floods, and they hold all the memory and knowledge that comes with it. Eternity sits in my hand, and it ties me to home.

Thinking about my experience of going home, I wonder about those who can't return to the lands that would remember them. Migrants like my maternal family who, in fleeing violence, are forever cut off from the land that knew them by the oppressive politics of those who hold power. Or those of the Black diaspora: people forcibly displanted again and again, people who may not even know which land held their ancestors.

But the land is alive, and perhaps the lands that exist in the place we call Africa carried stories of ancestors to its western shore.

Maybe the stories traveled on mycelium networks that stretch for miles underground. Maybe the trees whispered to each other. Maybe memories and knowledge were carried on the dust that blows from the Sahara across the Atlantic. Perhaps the sea, a primeval creature of long memory, accepted the burden of these stories and bore them on waves, gathering them along with the heartbeats and tears of those who did not complete the crossing. In this way, stories wash up on the shore of the land we call North America and are carried inland. The stories are shared in low murmurings, in the whispers of wind on trees and grassland, so that the beings who live here and listen carefully to such stories are able to offer medicine and belonging to those in diaspora.

Native people will tell you: *look for the medicine that shows up.*

I asked my friend Kerry, whose ancestors came across the Middle Passage to the Caribbean and then eventually to Canada, what medicine shows up for her. She said she feels called to the water. The waters of the Great Lakes carried Paddle-to-the-Sea all the way from Nipigon to the Atlantic Ocean. Maybe the waters carry the knowledge of her back to her ancestors.

We can't talk about restoring relationship to land without talking about restoring it to the people from whom it was taken. As a phrase, *Land Back* started with a tweet, which became a hashtag, which became a rallying cry for a movement of land restoration and Indigenous sovereignty. The movement has been in existence for hundreds of years; it's just that we now call it *Land Back*. For as long as colonists and their governments around the world have taken Indigenous land for themselves, we have sought to be restored to it. So we cannot talk about restoring our relationship to the land without talking about restoring the land to relationship with the people from whom it was taken.

The Karuk people, a tribe in northern California whose name literally means "the ones who fix the world," are provided as a case study in *Salmon and Acorns Feed Our People* by white academic Kari Marie Norgaard. In her book, she details the impact that loss of land has had on the Karuk people and how they are restoring both their landholdings and the ways in which they shape the environment. They work with fire in a kind of pyro-epistemology, like what Paulette Steeves describes, to manage their environment. This protects the waterways, which in turn provides salmon, as all these things are interconnected. Food sovereignty, which is tied to land, is a cycle of relationships, not just access. You drop one stone—say, by building a dam—and the unintended consequences ripple outward.

Settlers and migrants and the forcibly displanted get worried when Native people start talking about Land Back. What about their house? Where will they go? Unable to imagine any scenario other than what settler colonialism unleashed on us, people assume that Land Back means evictions, relocations, and elimination. In some cases, that might be appropriate. People own lakefront vacation homes that crowd Indigenous people out of traditional ricing beds, as documented in the play *Cottagers and Indians* by Drew Hayden Taylor. Luxury hotels and investment properties take up space, while Indigenous people are made homeless in their own territories. But wholesale eviction was never what we intended. Remember, from the earliest treaties, we offered a way to live together in peace, friendship, and respect. And although we are often, and I think reasonably, looking for change in ownership, at its core, Land Back means profoundly changing our relationship with land.

Because the Doctrine of Discovery gave European states the ability to claim whatever land they found, the land we lived on was no longer ours. Reservations aren't generally owned by the tribe that lives on them. The land is owned by the government and "held in reserve" for the specific use of Indigenous people. That is a precarious foundation for a community, as many tribes have experienced. The Wisconsin Menominee found themselves deemed "ready for termination" after achieving some economic success in the lumber industry, and in 1954, they lost their lands and their tribal status. The Menominee were reinstated in 1973, but the economic impact of termination was devastating.

Sometimes Native tribes identify particular places as sacred, perhaps in the hope that it will find some traction with those who are sympathetic to such things. But remember that the early colonists modeled themselves after ancient Israel's conquest of Canaan. Those early Israelites were commanded to "break down [Canaanite] altars and smash their sacred stones." So recognizing that Native places are sacred has never protected them from violence; in fact, it ensured it.

The US National Park system has been displacing Indigenous people for more than one hundred years. Just like governments use the language of safety, conservationists use the language of environmentalism to push aside the original peoples of the places where the parks now exist. In the 1960s, Minnesota senator Gaylord Nelson attempted to push through legislation that would remove waterfront land from the Bad River and Red Cliff Ojibwe reservations and turn it into a national park, moving the tribes further inland. Postwar prosperity meant family road trips and vacations for the middle class, and that meant increasing the available wilderness for them to travel *to*. Because of the engagement and activism of those tribal members, as well as the coordinated response from at least thirty other tribes and non-Native community members, this was unsuccessful.

In 2012, the Red Cliff Ojibwe opened Frog Bay Tribal National Park, which includes tribal lands as well as lands that they purchased from a retired professor. David Johnson learned that the tribe wanted to purchase the land he and his wife had bought decades earlier, but the tribe could not afford it. He sold it to them at half of its appraised value, saying that he had "always felt a little embarrassed at owning property that should have been in the tribe's hands all along." People can, and do, donate or sell property to tribal governments. It is one way that tribes are able to increase or restore their land base.

Actually restoring national parks to the Native peoples from whom they were taken is another idea that is gaining some interest in the United States and Canada. In the May 2021 issue of *The Atlantic*, Ojibwe writer David Treuer wrote a piece entitled "Return the National Parks to the Tribes." In it, he describes how the US government displaced the Miwok tribe from the land that would, thirty-nine years later, become Yosemite Park. This story repeats itself across the United States and Canada: Indigenous peoples banished from what conservationists saw as pristine wilderness. These parks were seen by settlers, in the words of David Treuer, as "natural cathedrals: protected landscapes where people could worship the sublime . . . an Eden untouched by humans and devoid of sin." But, he goes on to point out, these places were never untouched. In a reenactment of the fall, the settlers cast out the original people and called it pure. Treuer, and many others, argue that if the US government is to take seriously ideas of conservation and reconciliation, these lands should be placed under the control of the tribes from whom they were taken. He notes that there is precedent for this in Australia and New Zealand, where many significant natural landmarks are under the control of the Indigenous peoples: Uluru, for example, and almost half of the Northern Territory of Australia. In Canada, the territory of Nunavut was separated from the Northwest Territories in 1993 and is largely administered by the Inuit who make up most of the population.

In New Zealand, the Raupatu Lands component of the Waikato River claim was settled in 1995, and it returned land to the Maori tribe who had originally lived there, including lands that were under existing Crown ownership: the University of Waikato, Te Rapa Airforce Base, the Hamilton Courthouse, and the police station. These lands within the city boundary of Hamilton, New Zealand, are now Maori land. This arrangement has provided the Maori tribe with a tax base from which they can make decisions about development, and it involves them in a partnership with the city where they have real power to influence decisions.

What if the land responds to these claims? If it remembered me, does it remember others?

※    ※    ※

Somehow I made it through high school and college without reading John Steinbeck's *The Grapes of Wrath*. The book is about the migration of Okies, poor tenant farmers who were mostly but not always from Oklahoma. During the Great Depression, they followed Route 66 across the southern United States into California, where there were supposed to be jobs. In this passage, the squatting men are tenant farmers and have been told that they need to move out. The owners want the land, first to exhaust with cotton and then to sell to easterners who want to build houses on it. This passage, in which the bankers and tenant farmers argue over the land, felt so familiar, and it took my breath away. Steinbeck doesn't use quotation marks to separate speech, so I'll use italics for the words that the bankers say.

*You'll have to get off the land. The plows'll go through the dooryard.*

And now the squatting men stood up angrily. Grampa took up the land, and he had to kill the Indians and drive them away. And Pa was born here, and he killed weeds and snakes. Then a bad year came and he had to borrow a little money. An' we was born here. There in the door—our children born here. And Pa had to borrow money. The bank owned the land then, but we stayed and we got a little bit of what we raised.

*We know that—all that. It's not us, it's the bank. A bank isn't like a man. Or an owner with fifty thousand acres, he isn't like a man either. That's the monster.*

Sure, cried the tenant men, but it's our land. We measured it and broke it up. We were born on it, and we got killed on it, died on it. Even if it's no good, it's still ours. That's what makes it ours—being born on it, working it, dying on it. That makes ownership, not a paper with numbers on it.

*We're sorry. It's not us. It's the monster.*

When I heard this passage, I thought about how Steinbeck described relationship to land. These tenant farmers felt the connection—a connection that came through working on it, being born on it, dying for it and on it. Grandpa killed Indians. Pa killed weeds and snakes. They believed that the land was theirs because, like the earliest settlers, they worked it and drew sustenance from it. And just like the earliest settlers, they killed Indians in order to get it.

It's not us. It's the monster.

It's big brother, and he's hungry.

We're just the wendigo's victims.

In his moving and insightful novel about these tenant farmers, Steinbeck captures the cost of promises America makes and never intends to keep. The promise of land in Oklahoma. The promise of jobs in California. But he does it by vanishing Indigenous people and replacing us with the Joads and others like them. We used to be there, but in Steinbeck's world, we aren't anymore. Our presence is limited to an obstacle Grandpa removed. But surely Osage and Apache ancestors once squatted while colonists told them they had to move. Surely Cherokee ancestors insisted that it was our land, our children were born on it, we got killed on it, died on it. That's what made it ours: relationship, not a paper with numbers on it.

*The Grapes of Wrath* begins in Salisaw, Oklahoma. Recall that Oklahoma had been part of that vast geography into which the US government deposited all the Indians it didn't want living east of the Mississippi. These plains knew the Cherokee and Choctaw. They had longer memories of the Oceti Sakowin, also called the great Sioux Nation. Before that, this land knew the Wichita and the Caddo people, whose presence goes back at least two thousand years, through the mound builders. It knew the Osage. In *The Indigenous Paleolithic of the Western Hemisphere*, Paulette Steeves tells an Osage story, a fantastical story about giant beasts that had been dismissed as legend . . . until archeologists uncovered mammoth bones exactly where the Osage said they would be.

*When I say that the land is my ancestor, that is a scientific statement:* I want to reflect again on this claim by Dr. Keolu Fox, a Kānaka

Maoli anthropologist and genomic researcher. The land itself and
the conditions of that land, like altitude and climate, impact our
genome just as our human ancestors do. We are born on it, die on
it; we come from it and return to it. The land and the waters, oceans
and rivers, are part of us, relatives and ancestors in a very real way.
Inuk singer and activist Tanya Tagaq reminds me that the ocean is
the mother too.

Stones are also our relatives. Whatever I eat has taken up nutrients
from the ground, including minerals, and the land itself becomes
part of me. Thunderstorms and rivers become part of me. The land
and the waters have absorbed the blood and sweat of generations,
watched babies become old men and women and return to them. We
are part of each other. Civilizations rise and fall, and the land and
the waters continue. They hold memory of us all. Standing before a
presence that large and that old—and making one-sided claims of
ownership—is an act of extraordinary hubris.

Steinbeck's squatting men are calling on the land itself to witness
their plight. They aren't only arguing with the men who represent
the owners; they are appealing to the land itself to bear witness to
their presence, to their right of ownership. And the land is silent. It
does not put up any resistance or offer any comfort. Throughout *The
Grapes of Wrath*, the land bears silent witness to the destruction of
people and food, and it makes no response. Tractors plow the land,
and it offers up only dust. This is, of course, the time of the Dust
Bowl: a drought worsened by settlers who tore out the deep-rooted
prairie grasses and planted the land with thirsty, shallow-rooted
crops like wheat and cotton. In the same way, they tore out the deep-
rooted Native peoples and replaced them with newcomers.

During the drought of the 1930s, from Texas to Nebraska and up
into the Canadian prairie, high winds blew choking dust across the

region, killing people and livestock, covering fields that refused to produce even weeds and thorns. The land fasted and covered herself in dust.

Our emotions have a physical response. We feel sadness, and our body responds by crying. In the ancient Middle East, drought was often connected with mourning as *the land's* physical response to an emotional state. Just as a Hebrew mourner would fast and pour dust over their head and body, so, too, the land expresses her grief by fasting and covering herself in dust. "Human action has caused desolation and destruction," Mari Joerstad writes. "Further proof of human perfidy is *their inattentiveness to the suffering of other creatures.* The earth is left with no option but to cry directly to YHWH." The land mourns and wastes away not only because of the things that humanity has done but the things it has not done, such as our lack of care for those who suffer. The land has absorbed the blood of that suffering, and it mourns.

*We're sorry. It's not us. It's the monster.*

In ancient Hebrew texts, the prophets are not simply projecting their own emotions onto the world around them; they are recognizing and describing the emotions of the other-than-human world in which we all live and move and have our being. Land bears the scars and consequences of our foolishness long after we have passed. Land also lives in relationship to its Creator.

When I look at the chaotic weather patterns—at prolonged droughts and then at rain that falls out of sync with the needs of plants and without providing abundance—I know that human industry has had a hand in it. These are the result of things we have done, harms we have not cared about. Yet I cannot help but think that the land and the sea, the waters above and below, are responding as well. I wonder if, in response to our choices, the land itself is withdrawing in grief. Instead of giving us pathways that are lush and green, it is leaving us with charred landscapes that cut our feet. The writer of Leviticus warned Israel not to defile the land, or it would vomit them out. Anishinaabe ancestors warned us about the Seventh Fire and the path that would result from choices that the light-skinned people would make about how to live. Will that path be lush and green or black with char that cuts our feet? The land has more agency than we realize.

But all our stories contain mercy too. Solomon wrote that it rains on the just and the unjust alike. Eagles fly overhead, searching out those who are living in a good way. We can still listen to the stones that will surely cry out.

Do I really believe this?

"There was a time when I wondered—do I really believe all of this?" writes novelist Louise Erdrich. "I'm half German. Rational! Does this make any sense? After a while such questions stopped mattering. Believing or not believing, it was all the same. I found myself compelled to behave toward the world as if it contained sentient spiritual beings."

I don't know if the land is alive, not in the way that I know my dogs are alive. But it might be. And I've stopped bringing home rocks that don't belong to me.

❈   ❈   ❈

We need a reconfigured relationship, one that is reciprocal and recognizes the limits and hubris of ownership, the limits of a colonial way of living that destroys in order to replace. When the colonists originally came to the land they eventually called America, they saw themselves as latter-day Abrahams, as Israelites coming to a new Promised Land. But these are two very different ways of entering the land, and the colonists missed a key point about the early Hebrews.

First, Abraham did not enter as a conqueror; he entered as a supplicant, as a guest. Abraham lived among the people of Canaan, and when God said he would destroy the city of Sodom, Abraham argued with him, pleading for justice. Second, as Willie James Jennings writes, when the Hebrews returned to the Promised Land after centuries in Egypt, it was God who asserted sovereignty over the land, not the people. They developed a relationship with it, but the land itself belonged to God. These colonizing Christians took the conquest of Canaan as their model but not the form of land ownership that was instituted immediately afterward.

The practice of jubilee—restoring land to the original families—asserts both the temporary nature of our ownership and the enduring nature of the Creator's sovereignty. Our connection to the land is in our relationship with it, not our ownership of it. When we make it a thing that we can buy and sell, we not only sever our relationship with it; we sever it from its relationship with the Creator. That is something we should all take seriously.

Restored relationship is always a possibility, and exile is not forever. The Year of Jubilee is long past, and it is time to restore the land to the original people. In the United States and Canada, institutions are beginning to talk about improving relationships between institutions and Indigenous peoples. They call it "decolonizing." Churches, colleges, and settler organizations are beginning to recognize the colonial history of these countries and are trying to improve their relationships with Indigenous peoples. But *decolonizing* is not another word for anti-racism or anti-oppression; it is not just another way of saying *diversity* and *inclusion*. As Eve Tuck and K. Wayne

Yang remind us, decolonization is not a metaphor. We could be the most anti-racist society on earth, but as long as America relies on stolen land and the displacement of Indigenous people, it will remain a colonial state.

Decolonizing means returning the land to the people from whom it was taken.

As a thought experiment, I want you to think about what would happen if churches and businesses returned their land to the Indigenous people from whom it was taken. They would run the risk of eviction, that's true. But how would it change their behavior now that they are motivated to avoid eviction? How would churches act toward Indigenous peoples to ensure that their yearly lease gets renewed? What practices would businesses put into place to keep their place? How would that change in ownership change priorities? What ripples would that have in the broader community?

We must listen to the stones and what they might be telling us. We must listen to and acknowledge the land's grief. At the very least, we must stop participating in policies and practices that enact or entrench further displacement.

In *Salmon and Acorns Feed Our People*, Norgaard notes that early racial theorists included land in their analysis of how racism was developed and maintained. Theorists like W. E. B. Du Bois wrote about the importance of land in discussions about wealth and poverty. Contemporary theorists see inequity as lack of access to social resources. They talk about racism in our social structures rather than also analyzing land ownership itself. And that is interesting to me because by disconnecting inequity from access to land, any social justice action that we take reinforces settler colonialism. We're simply making settler colonialism fairer and more just, which means that our movements are built on Indigenous erasure.

Indigenous peoples often speak of belonging to the land. We say that the land owns us. It was into this kind of relationship that God invited the Israelites, and it was into this kind of relationship that the Haudenosaunee invited the Dutch when they made the Two Row Wampum treaty. The Year of Jubilee was more than an economic reset to prevent the accumulation of wealth; it restored each family's relationship to the land of their forebears and reminded the people that they did not own the fields that they purchased.

The land mourns, but it also responds with joy. The same prophets who describe a land fasting and covering herself with dust in response to human wrongdoing and harm also describe beautiful scenes of rejoicing and jubilation upon the return of the people. "The desert and the parched land will be glad; the wilderness will rejoice and blossom," the prophet Isaiah says.

Remember the two paths of the Seventh Fire—one parched and blackened and the other green and lush. How we prepare now will determine what comes next: either a healing fire that brings wild strawberries and lush pathways or a charred landscape that cuts our feet. For Indigenous people, that means holding on to the knowledge of our ancestors. For the light-skinned people, that means making the right choices about how to live.

These governments that make decisions? They are your model, not ours. This economic system we live under? This is your model, not ours. The Doctrine of Discovery that declared our lands were empty? That is your framework, not ours. You have choices to make.

## Aambe

It's one thing to consider our relationship with the land—our kinship to it—as individuals. We read books like Robin Wall Kimmerer's *Braiding Sweetgrass*, which is a lovely book and one you should definitely read. Reading books in solitude may alter our individual relationship with the world around us. But like our histories, our lives do not unfold in isolation. We exist collectively: as neighbors and community groups, as workplaces and sports teams, as book groups and families. We exist in overlapping relationships with faith communities and cultural groups: places and people with whom we have reciprocal relationship and with whom we can act together.

Seeding Sovereignty is an Indigenous-led collective that invests in Indigenous people and communities. Check out their website (seedingsovereignty.org) and the work that they are doing. Find other Indigenous-led organizations that may be doing work in your community.

How can you, as an individual and as part of a group, support one of these organizations? How can you join with them to do the things that need to be done?

## CHAPTER 7

# THE PEOPLE: WE ARE RELATED

One day, Nanaboozhoo was walking along the shoreline. He was hungry, and he looked for a way to get food without working too hard. He saw some ducks. He liked roasted duck, so he came up with a plan. Nanaboozhoo called out to the ducks, "Come over here. I want to sing you a song." The ducks were cautious but also curious, and they came over.

Nanaboozhoo told them to keep their eyes closed while he sang. Just listen to the song and the drum, he said, but keep your eyes closed, or the power will be lost. While the birds danced the shut-eye dance, Nanaboozhoo grabbed one duck, and wringing its neck, he threw it into the fire. Nanaboozhoo kept singing and drumming, and the ducks, with their eyes shut, kept dancing. Nanaboozhoo soon had six ducks roasting in the fire.

Eventually one of the ducks who was still dancing peeked. Maybe she was suspicious, or maybe it was just hard to keep her eyes closed that long. In any case, she saw what Nanaboozhoo was doing and called out a warning. The remaining ducks opened their eyes and flew away. Nanaboozhoo was angry and chased after them. When he got back to the fire, the ducks he was roasting had burnt, and he wound up with nothing.

This is a story about a lot of different things. It's about being lazy and trying to get something without working for it. But it's also about our own willingness to keep our eyes closed to what is happening around us—to enjoy the things we have without paying attention to what they might be costing others. That is why the tasks in the first part of the book have asked you to notice.

Notice marginalized people.
Notice the land.
Notice the agreements.
Notice the names.
Notice the absences.
*Notice the gaps.*

And now that we have noticed—now that we have opened our eyes from this shut-eye dance—we are rebuilding these relationships and thinking about what it means to be not only a relative but a good relative to the land and each other.

We are related, and all of our creation stories make that point one way or another. So the question has never been *whether* we are related but *how* we live out these relationships with the land, and with other-than-human relatives, and with each other.

After Nanaboozhoo was grown, he set out on a journey to travel the world and meet people, learning and listening and sometimes getting into trouble along the way. After he came back and told the Creator everything he had seen and learned, the Creator sent him out again, this time with a wolf as a companion. So Nanaboozhoo saw the world again, but this time, he saw it in relationship with another. Because that is how we best learn and how we are meant to live. In relationship.

When my oldest son lived in St. Catharines, Ontario, he had a house in a neighborhood that the larger community had marginalized.

Cities do this, marginalizing neighborhoods by not investing in their infrastructure, by how they zone it and nearby areas, by what does or does not get built there. Like Nanaboozhoo and the wolf, my son and his dog walked through their neighborhood, noticing the names and relationships. More than that, though, they formed relationships, and they formed connections. The neighborhood was tucked off to the side of the downtown area, and a reputation for drug deals and prostitution formed a barrier between this neighborhood and the bright lights. He had a garden in the back of his house that became a community garden. Some kids who lived nearby came over to see what he was doing, and he put them to work. A man who was intermittently homeless befriended my son and his garden, applying his knowledge about soil and plants to this small yard. People took and gave what they could, and somehow this scrubby yard in a scrubby neighborhood became a community.

We have begun to unravel the history we have been taught, unforgetting our relationships with this place and each other. We are challenging the myths that we were told about ourselves and each other, and we are learning the language to transform and confront settler colonialism. But there is no magic bullet. No single book you can read, no one podcast to listen to, no perfect Twitterati to follow, no percentage you can donate, and no amount of time you can spend outside in nature will put things right. We have to build relationships.

Naomi Klein has said that it is not enough to say that this is Indigenous land. We have to *act* like it is. Living as if the land belonged to the people we acknowledge means forming and working through relationships. Now we're going to unpack what it means to live together, to become kin.

Becoming kin often begins with having difficult conversations, and being willing to listen to the things marginalized people, the ones we are so used to helping, have to say can be difficult. It is one thing to help those who need help, but having conversations with the people around me about injustice in our community? Listening to them talk about their experience of injustice? That was hard. Maybe that's why we like charity and short-term mission trips, voluntourism that takes us far from home to where people who aren't like us need our help, need our generosity. And then we go home, thankful for our blessings, thankful that we aren't them. But you have to begin where you are, you have to organize the people around you, and that means listening to the people you want to help.

Some things are difficult to hear not only because they are upsetting, in and of themselves, but because they challenge things about the way that we interact with people and point out harms that we do. Helping feels good, but it is paternal; without relationship, it embeds hierarchy. The conversations that lead to kinship feel personal because they *are* personal. Relationships are personal, even professional ones, and I had to begin with the people around me.

Several years ago while I was still working in child welfare, I went to an academic conference aimed at helping participants decolonize spaces, including spaces where the work of education, social work, and other professions takes place. One of the workshops challenged the participants to talk with our racially marginalized clients about race.

Over my years in child welfare, I worked with a number of families who were racially marginalized. Bringing up race with them felt uncomfortable at first—which is odd, considering the kind of intrusive questions I had gotten used to asking in the context of doing my job. I could ask people questions about personal relationships, sexual relationships, physical abuse, mental health disorders. I could talk easily about any of these things with my clients, but we had never talked about race. In retrospect, it seems strange.

But as I began bringing up race, it got easier. And for them, it was like opening floodgates. These were clearly conversations that my racially marginalized clients, both parents and children, wanted to have. There were things they wanted to explain to someone—about their experiences in school, with other social-work organizations, and with child welfare in particular—but nobody had ever asked them. A six-year-old told me that he doesn't like Scooby Doo cartoons because "everyone is white except Scooby, and he's a dog." A fourteen-year-old said that he notices the way that old women look at him, the way they change where they carry their purse when he walks by. One day, after the topic of race had become a normal part of our conversations, an eleven-year-old told me about overhearing his teachers' comments about his younger brother's hair—how much tidier it would look if his afro was shorter. He told me how it made him feel.

Sometimes the answers were more challenging. "You saw a Black man here and assumed that he was my ex," someone told me once. "I didn't want to tell you I was Native because I know how child welfare sees Native families," said another—and then harshly, skeptically, "If you are Native, why are you working for *them*?"

Being confronted with racist ideas or behavior—our own or in the systems we're part of—is hard, but it is not the worst thing. The worst thing is being unwilling to listen, unwilling to do better.

One day during that time, as I was becoming more comfortable bringing up race, I asked my friend and eventual podcast cohost Kerry how she protects her dark Caribbean grandchildren who are going to a majority white school. She told me that she couldn't.

I wanted to know how she helped them withstand the inevitable racism they would experience, both the overt expressions that most people recognize and also the so-called microaggressions: how Black people are often represented (or not) in books or classrooms, the questions about their hair, and other ways that whiteness works to diminish Black and Indigenous children. When Kerry said that she couldn't protect them, my social-work brain went to the only vocabulary it had, so I asked her how she "builds resilience" in them. She leaned forward and smiled; she began talking about ancestors and the family stories she shares with her grandchildren. She talked about the connections that form, forward and backward and sideways across families and neighborhoods. She talked about communities that have come together, these diasporic people becoming kin.

We've been talking about it ever since.

*Aanikoobijigan* is the Ojibwe word for "great-grandparent" or "ancestor." But it is also the word for "great-grandchild" or "descendant." The word I would use to describe the person three generations before me and the person three generations after me is the same word and it connects seven generations. *Aanikaw*, the root word, refers to the act of binding or joining. Depending on prefix and suffix, this root can become a variety of words used to describe the sewing or tying together of the things.

So when I use *aanikoobijigan* to describe my great-grandparents, I am stitching, or tying, myself together with them. And when I use it to think about great-grandchildren not yet born, I am stitching myself to them too, tying us all together. When I see generations in my mind, I see threads that connect me to eight great-grandparents and then extend from me to children yet unborn. And when I look at my spouse, I see his threads connecting to eight others. My children's threads connect to my grandparents and to his, creating these webs of relationship contained within aanikoobijigan.

My hand drum is a piece of hide stretched over a wooden hoop. The sinew lacing on the back serves to keep the skin taut and provides me with something to hold on to while I play. For this drum, the sinew is woven in the style of a dream catcher, with a wooden bead in the center. That is what I see when I think about aanikoobijigan: each of us a bead at the center of a web that reaches out to connect us to so many others. Each one of us is surrounded by webs of relationship and connection. My drum is part of my bundle, a tangible thing, and through it I know relationship to my cousin who made my drum, my relatives who were there when it was given to me, my friends I sing with, the deer whose hide is stretched upon it, the tree whose wood forms the hoop, the fire and stars that witnessed the gifting. Like the water that flows from Lac Seul to the Great Lakes and past me to the sea, this drum connects me to the reserve where it was made and to Niagara, where it is played. These webs of connection stretch out, reaching to other webs, and collectively we hold the world together.

In her book *As We Have Always Done*, Michi Saagiig Nishaabeg author and artist Leanne Betasamosake Simpson writes about the importance of thinking backward and forward at the same time. Thinking in cyclical rather than linear time, we see more clearly the ways that generations are linked. We are so used to thinking of history in a linear way. But there are things we do every year, at a particular time, that return us to cycles. Annual holidays and gatherings are a way of marking cyclical time as we come back to those places and meals and specific family gatherings again and again. Each cycle brings us closer to the time when certain family members will no longer be present and new ones will. These spots in the cycle, feasts and gatherings, are thin places where past and future generations are tied together.

As part of this web connecting ancestors and descendants, we hold together these kin relationships in our lives. Each generation is doubling and extending behind me, in a vast web of relationships of cousins and aunties that connect me with other geographies and memories. Then there are our collective ancestors, who belong not only to me and my children but to the community itself, to the land itself. These are ancestors whose bones lie entwined with others beneath the ground and whose weaving holds this place together and emerges as medicine where we need it.

This is how Kerry "builds resilience" in her children and grand-children: through the sacred and precious items in her home, she tells them stories, of both specific relatives and collective ancestors, and the journeys they made across land and sea. She nests them in rela-tionships with living relatives and community members, as well as those they can only know through story, and together they become part of this web of stories and relationship that extend far beyond flesh and blood. Through these relationships and connections, the children are able to face the realities of the world that my young clients described to me and know who they are.

Thinking about these webs of relationships is part of picking up your own bundle. Think of something precious in your bundle, one of those things you would take with you if you had to flee. Look carefully at it and consider everyone whom that object connects you with. Sit with it in your hand and let this object speak to you of relationships and time.

And one day, we will be ancestors. What will our descendants know about us?

Aanikoobijigan.

As we think about what it means to become kin, it is important to think about what it *isn't*. We saw in *The Last of the Mohicans* and then later in *The Grapes of Wrath* how settlers tried to find belonging by appealing to their relationship with land, a relationship that either replaced or simply ignored Indigenous presence. These books are fiction, but fiction describes how we live and think. In *Not "A Nation of Immigrants,"* Roxanne Dunbar-Ortiz unpacks similar claims sometimes made by settlers in Appalachia. She observes that J. D. Vance's memoir *Hillbilly Elegy* describes Scots-Irish settlers finding belonging in the mountains that reminded them of home—and the way this belonging exists without Indigenous people, who were moved off these mountains, and without Black people, whose labor made these states possible. Vance identifies with a white ethnicity that works to separate itself from the elite but doesn't recognize its own participation in the erasure of others. Calling his people *hillbillies* allows them to take on the role of a downtrodden minority without taking responsibility for their role in colonization. Dunbar-Ortiz also describes ranchers in the West making claims to the land by virtue of working on it, living and dying on it. She contrasts the federal government's treatment of the Cliven Bundy family's occupation of Bureau of Land Management lands in eastern Oregon with the state's response to the Oceti Sakowin at Standing Rock to protest the Dakota Access Pipeline. The Bundys were handled carefully, while the Natives faced attack dogs and water cannons. This is not inconsistency; this is settler colonialism at work. And for all that Vance and the Bundys claim the land, this is not kinship with the land or with people; this is erasure.

Becoming good relatives, for settlers, is also not about becoming Native. Some white settlers seek belonging by looking for Native ancestry, which is another form of erasure. *Race shifting* refers to the act of people claiming Native identity based on an insubstantial, imagined, or invented connection to Native communities. They *shift* their racial understanding of themselves from white to Native. As DNA testing gains popularity, many scour their family tree for that one ancestor—that one of eight or sixteen or thirty-two or sixty-four grandparents, depending on how far back they need to go—who will make them Native, even though they have no familial relationship with an existing community. Maybe they heard a myth of a great-grandparent who was an Indian and wouldn't talk about it, or somebody remarked on their cheekbones or some other physical trait that "looked Indian." So like Elizabeth Warren was goaded into doing, they pay for an ancestry DNA test to tell them if the myths are true.

But the tests are flawed because, as Kim TallBear says in her book *Native American DNA: Tribal Belonging and the False Promise of Genetic Science*, they rely on ideas about racial purity that have their roots in medieval Spain and the *limpeza de sangre*, a belief that intermarriage with non-Christians, or new converts, could taint the pure blood of those who had been Christian for many generations. This belief in pure blood eventually became racial purity, and TallBear questions how that purity gets measured from a genetic standpoint. For example, who are the "pure" tribal members who get sampled in order to determine the markers that will identify Anishinaabe or Cherokee or any tribal group? There is, TallBear writes, no such thing as Native American DNA.

DNA is very good at identifying family relationships. It will tell you if somebody is a parent or a sibling, and it can even identify cousins and other relationships. But it is not good at identifying race because race is not biological; it is not encoded in our DNA. When geneticists look at our DNA, they see patterns or markers. Then they compare those with people in a particular area and see what patterns or markers are common in the people who were tested and also live in that area. If you have enough markers, these tests claim, then you are probably from a particular area. Probably, but not definitely. This is a precarious and self-interested identity that lacks the solid grounding of relationship.

I know that my great-grandfather was Irish, so a DNA test would probably prove that I have markers consistent with Ireland. But I have no connection to any Irish community, let alone the one in Clones, a town in western County Monaghan, Ireland, where his family was most likely from. It would be absurd for me to decide that, based on Isaiah, I am Irish.

A few years ago, an initiative sought to draw the Irish diaspora back to Ireland for a series of events. It seemed like a beautiful, affirming thing to me, and I said as much to a friend who is Irish. No, she said; it is marketing. This large-scale tourism push would actually displace the poorest Irish people, while people like me with family stories but no lived connection to Ireland—no connection to the political struggles and social realities of Ireland—came home and played at being Irish for a week or two. I thought about how they would certainly be welcomed everywhere they went, welcomed by those whose jobs or businesses relied on tourist dollars and the goodwill of those who are from away. And I remembered my own years working in the tourist sector. I remembered waiting tables and selling T-shirts, trading smiles and welcome for good tips. I also remembered being a tourist and how different cities look when you go one block away from the shining lights.

As Native peoples, we exist both as political and social entities. We have tribal citizenship rules that are set by governments and determine legal belonging. But we also have social relationships: family to whom we are connected or disconnected and the belonging those connections create. Those two ways of belonging overlap, but they are not the same. Belonging involves a reciprocity of claiming and being claimed, of responsibility to the community and community's responsibility to me. Of seeing and being seen. An individual race-based identity built on a long-ago ancestor or family lore is not that kinship-based relationship that is central to Indigenous belonging. It is a move to innocence—a way of not being a settler. A way of trying to be one of the oppressed rather than the oppressor.

It isn't wrong to think about your ancestors, to hear their stories and understand where they came from. And if your ancestors have been in the United States or Canada for a long period of time, it is possible that there is a Native ancestor back there. And if you have a Native ancestor—somebody who married or moved out of their community by choice or by force—it is understandable that you would want to know more about them, more about how they left and why, like Metoaka, they didn't return to their communities and instead remained among the colonists. Matt, a white Twitter user who goes by @Witch_of_SoCo, wrote about himself and his family tree: "Choices were made that put us on the side of the colonizer and we have to sit with that instead of pretending it didn't happen." He had found out that he had Native ancestry and "went through a phase" where he thought that made him Indigenous. But over time, he realized that although he had made friends within the Native community, he lacked that web of family relationships that connect generations. "Your ancestors are always your ancestors," he wrote, "but their communities may not be your communities."

In a similar vein, a coworker once started a conversation with me by saying that her great-grandfather was Native—possibly Mohawk, but she wasn't sure. Nobody in the family had any relationship with a Mohawk community. As I braced myself for the self-Indigenizing that often follows these statements, she said that she tries to be a good ally to Indigenous people by supporting actions that restore them to land or return children to families. She said that she felt this was the best way she could honor him and his experiences. I agree with her and with Matt. Our ancestors' communities are not always our communities, but we can build relationship with each other and honor our ancestors in that way.

This self-Indigenizing is not the same thing as the emotionally difficult journeys home taken by those who were adopted or stolen in child welfare scoops. For these children, now adults, their lived relationship is that deliberate policy of disruption. Their parents had relationships with others in the community, and their grandparents had relationships. There is an entire web connecting them with successive generations that they can reach out to. This is much different than scanning the horizon for a single relative many generations past.

My mother made a choice to raise me among settlers and apart from my Ojibwe relatives. Her decision wasn't malicious, but the harm was real, and I have to sit with that. I can't pretend it didn't happen or that it didn't insulate me from some things even as it failed to insulate me from others. Because of the way that others saw me—as the brown child in a white family—I had identity without relationships. That combination—identity with no community—impoverished me. That impoverishment was a constant hum in the background of my life. My face told a story that the rest of me couldn't articulate except as loss and absence.

So when people seek identity without relations, I find it baffling. Why would anyone seek that impoverishment? White people longing to discover a long-lost Indigenous ancestor likely don't *feel* that isolated identity like impoverishment, however, because their impoverishment comes from the systems around them. Colonialism works in all of us, to destroy and replace: destroying relationships and replacing them with isolated identities we can move around the country. It tells us to be one thing or another and never gives any of us time to be at home with ourselves. It tells us to be ourselves but then clearly lets us know which selves are welcome and which selves are not. Whatever we are is not enough, so we grasp for something else, as if that will imbue us with meaning. And it's empty because it isn't truly ours.

When I and other Native writers talk about being good relatives, we don't mean that you are distant cousins who somehow need to claim your indigeneity. Being good relatives means claiming your own ancestors—all of them. When you know who you are, when you are comfortable with who you are, you can enter into relationship *with* us rather than *as* us.

You can transform those ancestors who give you heartache, the ones who owned slaves or stole land, the ones who taught in residential schools or were members of the Ku Klux Klan (KKK). Aurora Levins Morales writes often about rejecting family mythologies in favor of telling her ancestors' true stories. Her great-great grandparents owned slaves, and the family mythology is that they were good to their slaves—kind slave owners. Aurora challenges this, as there is no kindness in slavery. She is an abolitionist, and her parents were both activists. This, she says, is how you transform these legacies you would rather not think about. You transform them by fighting against the things they, and you, benefited from, the legacy they gave you, not by transforming them into somebody they are not. She describes that possibility as truly transformative and profoundly hopeful, one that frees us all to act in ways that liberate everyone.

Aanikoobijigan: ancestors and descendants.

Nii'kinaaganaa: I am my relatives, *all* of them.

Thinking more broadly of relationships, I want to turn to settler colonialism—that process that destroys in order to replace—and consider it as something that shapes and controls our relationships to each other, to the land, and to our history. Settler colonialism is the structure that has forced our histories into silos, that pulled us apart and created gaps so that we do not see the things that were happening at the same time. It also forces our identities into silos so that we don't see each other. It offers us identity without relationship.

So we read *The Grapes of Wrath,* but we don't understand how the earlier settlers pulled out the prairie grasses and replaced them with thirsty and shallow-rooted wheat and corn the same way that Indigenous people were removed and replaced with tenant farmers. We don't realize that the displacement of the grasses and the people actually created the circumstances that displaced the Joads. We read the book or watch the movie *Hillbilly Elegy* and don't think about the Cherokee and Creek, who were pushed out of the mountains so that these Scots-Irish could find belonging and roots. We forget that Grampa killed Indians so he could have land. Settler colonialism betrays relationship by atomizing our communities into individuals, constantly making us into strangers by the divisions and constant relocations in our society.

Sara Ahmed writes about this in *Living a Feminist Life,* in which she reflects on how strangers are those who are "made strange" by the structures and assumptions around them. To be identified as a "stranger" is to be identified as not from here. A stranger is somebody who endangers those who *are* from here; strangers are being made dangerous because they are made strange. Made strange because you are made a stranger.

Ahmed's writing plays with words, using their multiple meanings to get at her point. Anyone who is racially marginalized has had the experience of being asked where they are from. If I say I am from Niagara Falls, the follow-up question is inevitably "Yeah, but where are you *from*?" I usually respond with "Thunder Bay," because that's where I was born. Often the questioner, who has read my ambiguously darker skin as meaning I'm not from "here"—not from Canada—gets increasingly frustrated. No, but where are you *from*? My darker skin makes me a stranger, not from here, possibly dangerous. People whose skin color or religion marks them as migrants, whether they are Black or Muslim, Asian or Mexican, often have a similar experience—but where are you *from*?—even though many in these diasporic communities have been "from here" for hundreds of years. Even though many Native people are also Black, or Muslim, or Asian, or Mexican and have been "from here" for a very long time.

At what point did light skin become an indicator of being "from here" and the skin of the original people become an indicator of strangeness?

※   ※   ※

Becoming kin means forming relationships that connect our communities. A number of years ago, a group of women, Native and non-Native, started to gather at the Fort Erie Native Friendship Center to sing and drum together. It began as part of a program for young mothers but quickly became a weekly gathering of its own. It's been five years now, maybe six, of people coming and going and coming back. The circle is a stable place of welcome in an unstable world—a place where the line drawn around us renders strangers into "sister-friends," as one of the members, a Choctaw woman we call Okie, is prone to say. Whatever social position we occupy out there, that meaning drops off in here, where we sit in a circle and where our only leader is the one who knows the song best. That's usually Sabrina, and we often look to her for teachings and guidance. For many of us, this circle is the closest we come to home.

There are several stories of how the hand drum came to the Cree, or to the Anishinaabe, or to whomever is telling the story. The story I learned is about a mother and daughter who were very close. They spent all their time together, gathering medicines and singing and taking care of each other and their community. The daughter died. The mother was inconsolable. One night, the mother was out looking at the stars—because we understand that we came from the stars and that we go back to them when we are finished here—and she saw the northern lights dancing in the sky. These lights took the form of her daughter and held her close. They gave her the drum and taught her to play it, striking the hide in a way that evokes a heartbeat. And the mother and daughter remain connected.

Aanikoobijigan.

One of the things that I like best about this drum group—and I like countless things—is that everyone has the opportunity to sing. Many of the songs have a similar structure, with a call and response at the beginning, followed by a verse that is repeated around the circle. Many of our songs have sounds or vocables—syllables that don't have set meanings—rather than words. I was told that this made our

songs universal; we could sing them with anyone because the vocables created a common language. These sounds also mimic our first
sounds, that cry we give as infants for our mother. These songs are
cries to our Mother, the Earth.

The first line is sung as a lead, or call, and then the rest of the
group sings it back, as if the first singer is saying, "Hey, where are
you?" and the rest call back, "We're here, with you." We often take a
turn singing that first line of a song. Sometimes the singer will mess
it up by singing too high or too low, singing it wrong, or forgetting
altogether. The rest of the group responds with the callback anyway,
drawing the singer back into the group—sometimes with laughter,
if the error was particularly spectacular, but affectionate, welcoming
laughter. And if somebody is afraid to try, whoever is nearby will
sing it with them to give them confidence. I love that because our
willingness to make mistakes encourages everyone to try. In trying,
you become part of that group of sister-friends who share something
magical.

The Roman world in which the apostle Paul lived, and after which
the early colonists and political leaders who shaped our current world
modeled themselves, was a world with rigid social hierarchies. Then,
as now, your rights (or lack of rights) were associated with your social
position: Black or white, landowner or tenant, Indigenous or settler.
These things don't stop existing when people enter into new relationships. When Paul wrote that there was "neither Greek nor Jew, male
nor female," it wasn't that people stopped being those things. These
things just stopped having social importance within the communities he was trying to build. The power or authority that some social
categories have was supposed to stay outside the church. Similarly,
the non-Native women who join the drumming circle don't *stop*
being non-native; they respect our teachings and practices without

needing to become us. We form a community of sister-friends. We become kin.

Aanikoobijigan.

We return to the idea of being claimed, because when we think about kinship and becoming kin, we generally think about who we *want* to be related to. But what about those we don't want to be related to? Whether it's ancestors we don't want to admit to having or larger social groups we don't want to be part of: what do we do with *unwanted* kin?

In her essay "*Claiming Bad Kin*," Alexis Shotwell, a white woman, considers this question. "White nationalists claim me, as a white person, as kin," she writes. "Though they may not know me personally, and though they would likely despair of my politics, they are working for a world in which I and white people like me hold citizenship . . . and are safe and flourishing." Then she wonders: what would happen if she claimed them back? What would it look like to claim them—not in the sense of accepting or condoning their belief system but as relatives? What if white supremacists are her unwanted kin: relatives who need to be addressed rather than simply disavowed and ignored, like family we turn away from at weddings or funerals? For her, this means challenging the beliefs when she sees them in her community, calling people into relationship and conversation. It means actively supporting the work of Indigenous people in reclaiming what was taken. And sometimes it means direct confrontation, like participating in counterdemonstrations when groups like the Proud Boys and others take to the streets. It means taking concrete steps to challenge a world in which she is safe but others are not.

Alexis Shotwell and Aurora Levins Morales offer us a helpful way forward as we consider our unwanted kin. "All of us inherit history," Shotwell writes; "the life we enter is a product of what has come before us. We inherit the life experiences of our ancestors as well as the material conditions in which those experiences unfolded. That inheritance sets the conditions for our individual lives." She continues: "We aren't personally responsible for the social relations and material conditions that came before us or that we enter in to, but we can become responsible for what we do in response to those conditions."

Levins Morales also writes about these legacies we inherit. In her essay "Raícism: Rootedness as Spiritual and Political Practice," she writes about acknowledging our ancestors' positions of power and then choosing to balance the books on their behalf as well as our own. We all, Black and Indigenous, settler and migrant, have at least one axis of power, and so while we gravitate toward those stories of being oppressed, it is important to acknowledge these other stories, particularly if those other stories make up most of your history. "Deciding that we are in fact accountable frees us to act. Acknowledging our ancestors' participation in the oppression of others (and this is true of everyone), and deciding to balance the accounts on their behalf and our own, leads to less shame and more integrity, less self-righteousness and more righteousness, more humility and compassion and sense of proportion."

We exist, just as the land does, with layers of overlapping claim. My Ojibwe relatives claim me. My drum group claims me. My German Ukrainian relatives claim me. The church claims me. The field of social work claims me. Canada claims me. These are not discrete categories, and there are many places of overlap and impact. There is no time at which I exist in only one of these relationships.

Many times before my maternal grandmother passed away, I sat with her and listened to her stories, how she and my grandfather were both pushed aside in their native Ukraine and able to find home. I can't look in her eyes and disavow her or pretend that we don't belong to each other as if I was only Ojibwe, somehow purely Indigenous. There is strength and resilience in her stories, powerful women whose legacies combine within me alongside my Ojibwe grandmothers, Lula and Sophie. There are creative grandfathers, resourceful and brilliant, whose legacies combine with Roy and Joe. I would be impoverished without them. Yet displaced as they were, they found home as the *result* of the displacement of the Michi Saagig Anishinaabeg. My maternal ancestors did not kill Indians like Grampa in *The Grapes of Wrath*, but they benefited from those who did. They found home within the settler-colonial state, not with Indigenous peoples, and so I carry that as well.

Neither can I pretend that I don't have relationship with the church or the field of social work just because I struggle with much of what they have done and continue to work toward. The social justice maxim to organize and speak with the people around me echoes in my ears, and I think about my responsibilities to all of my kin, wanted and unwanted.

Using the Doctrine of Discovery, the governments of the United States and Canada have described the land and its people as "empty." They use settlers to fill the land, and they use religion or social theories to fill the people. Settler colonialism does not notice what abundance is already there, what good news we might have to share that would help them. So what is my responsibility in these relationships? What is yours?

I did not create the policies that shaped what I did as a social worker or the theology that shaped my beliefs as a Christian. But we become responsible for what we do in response. We return to ourselves by picking up our bundles and taking responsibility for the relationships and material conditions we have inherited.

Biskaabiiyang.

It is important as settlers and as Indigenous people that we return to ourselves. Settlers often try to avoid this; I've written about how they sometimes try to *become* us and how harmful that is. It is also disrespectful to their own ancestors. Through my maternal family, I am also connected to those who may not have intended to displace Indigenous peoples but whose presence on our lands *did* displace us. Through my mother, I am connected to those who taught in residential schools. She did not teach in a residential school, but she did teach in a small Oji-Cree community not far from one. And she held many of the same ideas about "civilization" that those who taught in and administered those schools held. Sending white teachers north to teach the Indians is not the same as taking children from their families, but it still imposes colonial ideas about value and social position.

It may be that your settler ancestors suffered too. It's possible that they fled hardship and trauma as my maternal family did. But they had somewhere to flee *to*. Where were Indigenous people supposed to go in order to start over? As we have seen, there is a long history of Indian removals in Canada and the United States, but eventually the governments ran out of places to send us. So they started to eliminate us through residential schools and child welfare. After centuries of separating us from land, they turned their attention to separating us from each other.

Returning to yourself means understanding how your ancestors were used, wittingly or not, to displace and replace, and then working with us to ensure that we are safe from further displacement.

Here we must also look at the reality of those living in diaspora. Descendants of the enslaved did not come here fleeing trauma and hardship; they were disconnected from their land and brought here by force. They were brought here by force and then removed, again and again, in service to the colonial state. Removed again and again into prisons and poverty. They are also indigenous to this place through relationship. Black Natives are real and carry these threads of ancestry within them. Migrants fleeing the violence that the colonial West outsources to protect itself did not choose to abandon their homelands. But however you arrived, we must all choose how we will live here.

Returning to yourself means picking up those threads and working through what it means to find home in the place you were removed *to*. Dunbar-Ortiz ends *Not "A Nation of Immigrants"* with a call to those who have migrated or who are descended from migrants. She asks them to look past the myth of America as a nation of immigrants. She invites them to see the process of settler colonialism at work—the Americanization that they or their ancestors went through that erased Indigenous people's presence—and to then make a choice about how they will live. Immigrants move into a place and adapt themselves to an existing political system. Settlers impose their own system. Finding home on Indigenous land means living as if this is Indigenous land, not just saying it is.

In *Our Knowledge Is Not Primitive*, Wendy Makoons Geniusz writes about notebooks that Ojibwe elders kept about different forms of knowledge. In her case, she is writing about botanical and medicinal knowledge and the elders from whom she learned the things she now teaches. These notebooks were meant for personal use, and, as with any personal notebook, they contained a kind of shorthand that made sense to the writer. But more than that, she writes, the notebooks that older Ojibwe left behind about their knowledge and medicines often left out crucial information. This was strategic on their part, she claims. They left out some knowledge that, if those notebooks fell into unthinking or impulsive hands, could be misused.

You can't just read books about us. There are things that won't be there. In order to make sense of Indigenous knowledge, you need to invest the time and effort in relationships with people and communities.

When the first duck in the shut-eye dance opened her eyes, she began to question the story she had been told about this dance. When Abraham and Moses argued with God about the impending destruction of people, they were questioning the story they had been told about God himself. We must question the stories we have been told.

Biskaabiiyaang.

We return to ourselves.

## Aambe

Spend some time looking at timelines and visual histories. Charts like the Histomap show parallel histories of various cultures over thousands of years. So you can look at 1500 CE, for example, and see what was happening in Europe and Asia and Africa at the same time. These charts sometimes reveal relationships between things that we may not have noticed before.

To make a timeline or visual history of your family, take a moment to sketch out a family tree, the names, dates, and places as best as you can remember them. Don't worry about the gaps; you can use this to talk with other family members later and fill those in. Right now we're just making a broad sketch. You can do this with your profession or community group as well: sketch out its history from when it was formed to how it came to exist as you know it.

The book *Stories of Repair* is a compilation of stories from the Mennonite church in the United States and Canada that offers next steps in reparative justice. It suggests three questions that you can consider alongside these histories you have written down. Using the things you have learned throughout these chapters, create a parallel history with these questions:

1.  Who used to live in the place where your ancestors lived? Where your church is built? Where your profession emerged and now operates?
2.  How did they get displaced?
3.  Where are their descendants today?

These things—your relatives and their places in history—are your inheritance. These connections will shape your responsibility as we gather our bundles and move into thinking about solidarity.

# CHAPTER 8

# SOLIDARITY: BECOMING KIN

L ong ago, the deer abandoned the Anishinaabeg.

Humans are fragile creatures. We rely on everything that came before us in creation to protect us. In the Anishinaabe creation story, the animals and plants—and probably the rocks too—promised the Creator that they would take care of us. They welcomed us into creation, and in this way, they welcomed us into relationship.

But one day, the deer withdrew.

The Anishinaabeg were overhunting. We were being wasteful and greedy. Maybe it happened all of a sudden, or maybe it took some time, but one day the hunters went out . . . and nothing. This happened repeatedly, and eventually the people realized that the deer were gone. This withdrawal of the deer had consequences for other animals and plants that we relied on for food, and so anxiety filtered out of the camp and throughout the land. The other animals started misbehaving too—maybe getting cocky, maybe getting anxious about the changed world around them. Maybe they, too, thought about withdrawing as our reliance on them increased in the absence of the deer.

Over the winter, the people were hungry. Winter is the time for stories in Anishinaabe communities, as it is for so many others. Long nights of telling stories, which are actually memories, connect us to ourselves. The Osage kept stories about a battle between giant beasts. The Anishinaabeg and other tribes kept stories about thunderbirds. And of course, in the winter, we are thinking about the north. Giiwedin.

No doubt the people listened to stories of Nanaboozhoo. Maybe they listened to a story about the shut-eye dance and how Nanaboozhoo took more than he needed. Maybe they shifted uncomfortably in their seats. But these long nights of telling stories reminded the people who they are, reminded them about promises made and kept and broken. During these evenings, they were unforgetting.

In the spring, the people laid their tobacco on the ground as an offering, and they prayed and sang. Then they sent out runners in the four directions looking for the deer. These runners ran and ran, covering great distances, and one by one they returned. Nothing. Nothing. Nothing. Finally—maybe because this is how it is in stories—the last runner came back and said she had found one young deer, far to the north. This young one had told her that the deer had felt disrespected and threatened. So they left.

The young deer explained that initially they had waited to see if the humans would remember what we knew. But seeing from our behavior that we had no interest in relationship, and no interest in maintaining the agreements we had made with them, they left. This must have been a difficult decision because of the promise that they had made to the Creator that they would take care of us. The deer needed to think about their own survival, though. If we killed them all, they wouldn't be here to take care of us anyway.

The people sent their diplomats, their elders, and their ceremonial people to meet with the deer, and for as much time as it took, they listened. They listened to the stories and to the harm they had done.

They listened to old relationships and memory. They listened to how things should be. They made offerings and agreements.

Only then did the deer return to them. The people agreed to live in respect for the deer. They agreed to take care of the relationship that takes care of them.

Nii'kinaaganaa.

Biskaabiiyang.

Bimaadizowin.

I don't know what the deer did while they were gone. Maybe they relaxed for a while, knowing that they weren't being hunted. Maybe they sang whatever songs deer sing when we aren't there to hear them. They took the time that they needed, and they returned to themselves. Then, when they were ready, they sent one deer out to where the runner could find her.

Over the winter, before the people sent out runners, they, too, did work. Sometimes when we tell this story, we go right from the part about the people realizing the deer were gone to all of them sitting together. Sometimes we don't think enough about that long, hard winter.

By the time spring came and the people sent runners, we had remembered enough of ourselves to lay tobacco and to pray. All through the winter, we heard stories and sang songs. The absence of the deer would have changed how we heard some of these stories, how we felt when we sang some of our songs. We remembered our place in creation and our responsibilities to each other.

※   ※   ※

Perhaps, after reading this far, you are also starting to see some of your familiar stories and places differently, to hear some of your familiar songs differently. Maybe some of these stories and songs leave you feeling uncomfortable in a way that you had not felt before.

When the unmarked graves of children were exposed in the summer of 2021, people were understandably upset. Across Canada, Indigenous people took time apart to grieve these little ones. We lit fires and held ceremonies. Settlers also felt bad, but there wasn't anything they could do with their grief, and so they wanted to rush to reconciliation, they wanted to rush to apology and forgiveness. How can we help? What can we do? Many of the settler Canadians interviewed in the book *Living in Indigenous Sovereignty* talked about the impact that learning history from other perspectives has had on them. This unforgetting propels them to action. But what kind of action should come first? In his interview, Rick Wallace says that one useful act of solidarity is for settlers to talk with other settlers to help critique the history they have been taught and the relationships they have inherited. Talking with each other about what you are learning, challenging the histories you were told: it sounds like what the Anishinaabeg did during the winter, long before they went looking for the deer.

When my oldest was a very small child, he got into trouble like small children do. It was something he had done a hundred times before and something he would probably do a hundred times again. I was angry and frustrated. He looked up at me and said, "I said I was sorry; you have to forgive me." And I stopped, because I taught Sunday school to four-year-olds, and we had just done a lesson about Jesus telling one of his followers that he has to forgive his friend seventy times seven times. Maybe my oldest had heard my husband and me going over the lesson, or maybe he had it in his own Sunday school class, but his plea caught me off guard and made me laugh.

This very simplistic way of understanding apology and forgiveness is okay for small children, and it helped me move past my frustration with whatever it was he had done and would probably keep on doing. But it is not sufficient for adults. Yet when we talk about reconciliation with Indigenous people, that is exactly the way that we talk about it. There is a push for the Catholic Church to apologize for its role in residential schools. Other denominations in Canada have apologized. The government has apologized. And after the remains of hundreds of children were found outside one residential school after another after another in the summer of 2021, the demand for the Catholic Church to apologize heightened. But the way that settlers and Indigenous people think about apology and reconciliation is very different, and so we use the same language, but we don't mean the same thing. Churches and governments keep what they stole and tell us, "We said we're sorry; you have to forgive us."

In the chapter on spiritual growth in his book *Anishinaabe Ways of Knowing and Being*, Lawrence Gross writes about a conference on Native justice that took place in 1986 in Whitehorse, a city in the Canadian Yukon. Speakers and participants were looking at models for reconciliation in the context of the criminal justice system. The scenario under discussion at one workshop was one in which a young man had broken into a store and vandalized it. A group of community members gathered to develop strategies that would resolve the crime without putting the young man in jail. They role-played a mediation, which you may be familiar with as an alternative dispute strategy. Everyone had a chance to talk about what happened. The victim—the storeowner—talked about how the vandalism had impacted him, and the wrongdoer listened. They talked about how they felt about each other and what could be done to reconcile the two parties.

This sounds like a typical mediation activity: get the two sides together and let them talk in a safe environment. It may even sound like the meeting between the deer and the Anishinaabe. But wait.

An elder at this event told them that this was not how it would have been done traditionally. When we are quick to put people together in a conversation after harm has been done, the victim, who often still feels unsafe, may agree to a form of reconciliation that doesn't fully address the wrongs that were done. Rushing toward reconciliation without both parties being fully prepared often results in more harm, particularly when those rushing to repair are part of the dominant society, the settler class with the most political and social power.

This elder offered a different practice. In his scenario, the victim and the wrongdoer would each be taken under the responsibility of separate elders. The victim and the wrongdoer would meet regularly with their assigned elder and work through their respective feelings of victimization and entitlement, of grief and anger. In these separate meetings, they would sing songs, and they would do ceremony. Maybe they would do counseling, and maybe the wrongdoer would complete restitution. It is important for the victim to do the work as well; "hurt people hurt people," as the saying goes.

Throughout the process, the victim and wrongdoer, along with their assigned elders, would meet periodically with a peace pipe on the table between them. If one elder believed that their charge had resolved the matter—if they had returned to themselves—that elder would touch the pipe that was laid between them. Only when both elders touched the pipe would they smoke together, and the matter would be resolved. Then the victim and the wrongdoer together could be restored to the community and to each other.

This is what happened between the deer and the Anishinaabe. The deer took the time they needed to return to themselves, and when they were ready, they sent out a messenger to see what the Anishinaabe would do. Meanwhile, the Anishinaabe did not just sit and sulk—or maybe they did at first. But they also thought about what happened and what they may have done to cause the rupture. When they were ready, they sent out runners to seek a meeting. The Anishinaabe did more than just say they were sorry and expect that to be the end of it. They changed themselves, and they changed the relationship.

They became kin. Nii'kinaaganaa.

Lawrence Gross suggests that the Anishinaabe worldview is something like quantum physics. If you'll stay with me a moment, you'll see why this matters to our consideration of apology and reconciliation. As I told you, Anishinaabe is a verb-based language. In the Anishinaabe way of seeing and naming the world, we are *humans being*. But this applies elsewhere too. In Anishinaabe, my shirt is not blue; it is *being* blue. The rock is not hard; it is *being* hard. The things that we observe are not the inherent qualities of whatever we are looking at; the shirt or the rock is simply what it is being in this moment. This is a very quantum-mechanics way of thinking. Remember: light, depending on how you look at it, is both particle and wave. This applies to people as well.

That boy who vandalized the store is not a vandal. Vandalizing the store is something he *did*, not who he *is*. As I understand the way our language works, we could describe what he had done to the store, but we would not have a noun to attach to his identity as a result. What he did to the store is an action he took, not a core identity. Because his action in one place and time does not define him forever, he can admit his wrongdoing and do the work that he needs to do in order to ensure that he does not harm his community this way again.

There is always possibility for change; in fact, this capacity for change is integral to who we are. *Humans being.*

The elder's suggestion—that the boy and the storeowner do their own work with their own elders long before they sit down together—is significant. Like the deer and the Anishinaabe, like the young man and the shopkeeper, there's work to be done long before we sit down together. Reading this book has been part of that, thinking through our shared histories and how policies and laws developed. Each chapter has ended with a task that asks you to turn this learning inward—to look at your own community and your own relationships. To begin to talk with and organize the people around you.

I have used the language of settler and Native, colonizer and Indigenous. Sometimes people hear these words and get defensive: "I'm not a settler. I didn't colonize anything!" Race shifting, or trying to become Native, is one way to avoid the implied accusation and, by extension, the responsibilities.

And that response makes a certain kind of sense. Binaries are rarely accurate. They are useful containers in which to think about collective processes, but people don't always fit easily into these categories. I just spent time explaining that in the Anishinaabe worldview, the things we do don't define us forever. But I'm limited by English, which does describe people in this way. So let me reframe it.

Being a settler or a colonizer is not something you *are*; it is something you *do*. It describes your relationship to this land and the people in it. Remember that settlers come to impose a way of living on top of the existing people. Settler colonialism destroys in order to replace. If you are going to stop being a settler and start being kin, that's where we start. With what you do.

In her book, *The Land Is Not Empty*, Tewa descendant and academic Sarah Augustine writes about the Doctrine of Discovery and how people can work to dismantle it. She says that solidarity is not symbolic; it is not a gesture or a way to end a letter. Solidarity is actions we take that put us on the side of the oppressed and not the oppressor, that put us in relationship with the original people of this land rather than those who impose other systems on them.

My friend Liz is Miskito and a teacher-librarian in a public school. One of the things that she does is go through the books in her library, quietly removing the ones that diminish racially marginalized people and using her budget to purchase books that reflect more diversity. She does this not just so her marginalized students can see themselves as heroes or main characters but so the other students can as well. She tells them about the Indigenous people who aren't in the story so that they learn to look for what is not there.

Some churches and organizations have a budget line for donations to the tribe on whose land they have their church building, donations that come without strings or expectation. Others find ways of showing up to actions and events, providing physical support. In the winter and spring of 2017, after the United States used rubber bullets, tear gas, and water cannons on Indigenous Land Defenders at Standing Rock, US military veterans arrived to put themselves between the people and the military that opposed them.

Standing Rock may be the most well known of these types of actions, but you don't need to travel to South Dakota to show solidarity. Land Back actions are taking place in a variety of ways and places across the United States and Canada. We saw in the early chapters and revisited in chapter 6 how our relationship to the land is central to how we live, all of us. Land theft is not only the taking of land; it is the profound alteration of it through extraction rather than relationship. Land theft includes extracting water, extracting lumber, extracting minerals and animals and people. Indigenous peoples globally hold 80 percent of the world's biodiversity in about 22 percent of the land area. Indigenous land and Water Protectors are doing what they can, but we are only 5 percent of the world's population, and the land mass we do have is being eroded and impacted by the industries in the other 78 percent. There is mercury in the fish of northern Ontario—mercury that is there because of hydroelectric dams and paper mills. Mining that takes place far from my reserve puts toxic dust in the air that settles in the water and now waits in my freezer to be eaten with the walleye that my oldest son caught.

Sarah Augustine began her work among the Indigenous peoples of Suriname. She went in as a notetaker and found herself advocating for them at the United Nations and the World Council of Churches. The colonial processes of destroy and replace, of moving Indigenous people into villages and off the land, are still at work. People in Suriname are in the way of a mining conglomerate whose actions put mercury in their water. Augustine eventually founded the Dismantling the Doctrine of Discovery Coalition, and her organization provides many concrete things that people and organizations can do to pressure governments and corporations to change their policies.

Once we understand the structural nature of what is happening, Augustine writes, we can turn away from individual feelings of guilt for things we didn't do. Instead, she says, we can engage collectively with others to "dismantle the structures of inequity." What if churches sent missions to Wall Street?, she asks. To mining corporations? To Washington? What if churches sent missions to those who are enacting the harm and told them to stop? What if denominations worked together to demand change?

For too long, churches have been the foot soldiers of colonialism. Throughout the Global South, churches still often operate as advance forces, gathering Indigenous people into modern praying towns and off the land so that settlers and corporations can extract lumber or minerals, build a dam, or somehow extract money from the place where Indigenous people used to live. What if churches and people of faith turned their backs on that mission and embraced another?

If the Seventh Fire is going to result in a path that is lush and green, you are going to need to make choices about who you will be in solidarity with. Settlers and migrants need to decide where they fit in and how they are going to live here. Every business and organization seems to have a diversity and inclusion committee, but if we are going to talk about inclusion, we need to think about inclusion into *what*? Inclusion into a settler-colonial state built on the ongoing erasure and displacement of Indigenous people?

Now I want you to look for the places where we do gather and then go there. Don't wait for us to come to you. The Anishinaabe did not wait for the deer to return to them; they sent out runners. Some of those runners came back empty—but one did not. Remember what the Anishinaabe did when they sat down with the deer: they listened.

The book *Living in Indigenous Sovereignty*, by Elizabeth Carlson-Manathara and Gladys Rowe, is a collection of essays and interviews written by settlers who are working through what it means to become kin, live in solidarity with Indigenous people, and act as if the land truly belonged to us. In these essays and interviews, a number of settlers talk about how they began to show solidarity with Indigenous peoples. They describe realizations and relationships, successes and failures. Mostly they talk about showing up.

I often tell people to show up, and it really is that simple. Show up. Show up to protests and powwows. Show up to urban Indian centers when they have activities and events—most of them are open to the general public. Join their groups on social media. It may feel strange or awkward at first. Bring that friend with whom you are reading this book. Over time, you will become familiar and known. If you offer to wash dishes, you'll make friends that much faster.

In the foreword of *Living in Indigenous Sovereignty*, Aimée Craft, Leona Star, and Dawnis Kennedy write, "Too often the burden of decolonization is taken up by Indigenous people, or in effect placed on Indigenous people's shoulders." This burden is shared but not in the same way. We each have our own work to do—our own bundles to pick up. The people interviewed also talk about learning from relationship and then taking that learning back with them to their churches and civic groups, to their businesses and neighborhoods, and then organizing the people around them.

*Organizing* is a scary word. We hear it, and we think about large-scale events and mass mobilizations, but it begins with finding one person you can disrupt with. One person at work or at church, in your neighborhood or your community group. Together you can organize a book club. You can organize a letter-writing campaign. You can organize people to speak at city council meetings and provide support to politicians who are trying to do better. You can organize the collection of cold-weather gear for migrant workers coming from countries where they didn't need sweaters.

Even if you only find one person to disrupt with, you can support each other as you raise a concern about a decision your organization is making. If you are on a board, you can make a motion to add a budget line for reparations and have one person to second it. You find one person, and then you stick up for each other as you try to organize the others around you. Together you can follow Indigenous-led groups and movements into restoring what was stolen.

You can find ways to connect your community with ours. Churches, synagogues, mosques, and civic groups can offer support for protests and vigils by showing up, bringing water, paying for the rental of sound equipment, or covering parking fees. In early 2018 when verdicts in the deaths of Colten Boushie and Tina Fontaine came down within a week of each other, Black Lives Matter Toronto arranged to organize the second vigil so the Indigenous community in Toronto wouldn't have to. That same year, I was invited to speak at the one-year memorial for the victims of the 2017 mosque shooting in Quebec City. And in the summer of 2021, when vigils seemed to happen every week, an imam spoke words of comfort and peace at one of our vigils, and I spoke of solidarity at one for Palestine.

There is a mosque in Inuvik, a community in Canada north of the Arctic circle. In *Praying to the West*, Omar Mouallem talks about the members' relationship with the Inuit and migrants who call this town home. He quotes Abdalla, a Muslim man who runs a food bank and who says that their dawah (propagation of Muslim faith) is not by preaching; it happens by becoming part of the community, giving back to the community. Mouallem observes that "By allowing himself to be absorbed into Indigenous, and not settler Canada, and by becoming a vital member of it, Abdalla had earned both the Inuit's knowledge and welcome." This isn't a universal practice; elsewhere in the book there are examples of colonial behavior, of a hyper-patriotism likely born of a need to feel safe, to be the "good ones." But reading this, I had to wonder: what if Christians had entered Indigenous communities in this way five hundred years ago? What if Americans and Canadians, settlers and migrants, sought that kind of relationship today?

What would be possible?

I hope that this book leads to others. I have taken care in who I quote and reference, and there are other writers mentioned in the endnotes and Further Reading, as well as those in the Acknowledgments, whom I may not have quoted but whose work and writing have shaped my thinking. Work through the tasks together with others so that when the difficult emotions come, you have somebody to sit with. Be with someone as you let the floodwaters of history—and your ancestors' and your role in it—wash over you. That way you don't need to fear the waters of guilt or loss or grief. With the support of others, you can trust that you will surface, still breathing and holding on to a handful of mud with which to imagine and create something new.

I cannot stress relationships enough. This is important, but it is also not something to be jumped into. This is the last chapter of the book, not the first. It is important to enter into these relationships with humility and respect, having already begun the work of unforgetting. Yes, there are always more layers to unpack. But now you know how to look for us, how to question the things you are taught. You know how to listen differently, and hopefully you have some language to challenge others.

I have read a lot about the history and political activism of marginalized peoples, but it is friendships that shape my understanding of how they move through the world. It wasn't until I started listening to my clients about their experiences as racially marginalized people that I started to understand how my profession impacted them. And it was the work I did ahead of time that allowed me to hear and understand the things they were telling me without becoming defensive. That allowed me to move toward solidarity with them and becoming kin.

We started this book with looking for the Black and Indigenous people around you. We looked for them on your bookshelves and in your neighborhood, in your workplaces and your faith communities. We looked for their presence and their absence. And we end in the same spot: looking for them in our lives and in our relationships. We end by finding a new center to revolve around.

A song is where we started this journey—a song that contained grief and hope, loss and possibility. We began with footsteps walking onto a darkened stage, where a friend waited with me to remind people that we are still here, that we are still connected to this place through song and language. The wooden stage and the concrete sidewalks do not separate me from the Earth; they are part of the Earth. Taken and reshaped to another purpose, the Earth is still there, and I can feel her beneath my feet. The asphalt made of oil is, as my friend Zoe Todd reminds me, the remnants of dinosaur relatives. In this way, even the roads connect me to a distant past, although the making of these roads was certainly not a respectful way to treat our ancient relatives.

The roads and the waterways connect us to far-flung places, and to each other, carrying news of us perhaps to places that remember and long for us. Every item I have in my home connects me to the hands that made it, that packed it for transport, that stocked it on a shelf and scanned it for purchase. The piles of books that surround me and my endlessly scrolling Twitter feed are also forms of connection, a sharing of ideas and distractions.

Songs connect us to each other and across time. My drum group has sung for a friend's Native studies class, sitting around a fire with trees overhead and rocks beneath our feet—beings that perhaps remembered older songs. This is also connection. The call and response of our songs is a kind of reciprocal relationship, one that I hope you have heard in this book. Together we hear the call of history, and the future anticipates our response. We are related.

It is hard not to see that the invented history of the Western world is crumbling fast. Around us the floodwaters are rising. Wendigos and other hungers stalk our lands in three-piece suits and stand behind podiums, while each side argues over the merits of electing their particular monster.

So many people are still dancing that shut-eye dance, refusing to see or hear the harms of settler colonialism, something I hope is now obvious to you. Talk to the ones whose eyes are still shut. Put books into their hands. Become tiresome. The world is alive in ways we don't understand. The heavens pour out praise, and the trees clap with joy. And with a song and a handful of mud, we can make this world new. We can walk together on a good path that is green and beautiful and together we can light the eighth and final fire: an eternal fire of peace, love, and kinship.

Doing the work of picking up your own bundle, of returning to yourself, will help you move from being a settler to becoming kin. You'll see what you have to offer—because you do have things to offer.

We walk this path together, as the Two Row Wampum, that original treaty that the Haudenosaunee offered the settlers, lays out: each in our own way, but together.

Nii'kinaaganaa.

We are related.

## Aambe

Your final task is to organize the people around you. This is hard work, largely because you have changed and because the people around you know an earlier version. They liked that version. But now you know better; and as the saying goes, when you know better, you have to do better. It is important to honor these relationships and the possibility they contain. Organize the people around you.

Whatever you are angered by, outraged by, troubled by as a result of this book, there are people who are already doing that work and have been doing that work for a long time. Find them and join them, because when I say to organize the people around you, I don't mean that you should rush in to save us. Find groups that are led by Indigenous people.

Organize the people around you so that you can bring them with you—so you can share the good news of a green path lush with grass and a world of possibility.

# ACKNOWLEDGMENTS

My friend Maya likes to begin her workshops with a story about smart berries. Nanaboozhoo was known for many things, including wisdom, and people often sought him out, wanting to learn from him. One day, a particular Anishinaabe asked Nanaboozhoo how he got so smart, and Nanaboozhoo told him about smart berries. "Oh, where are these smart berries?" the Anishinaabe wanted to know. He begged and pleaded, and eventually Nanaboozhoo agreed to take him for a walk to where the smart berries were.

After a while, Nanaboozhoo stopped. Before them on the path was a scattering of berries on the ground. "There they are," he said, and in a flash, the Anishinaabe scooped up the smart berries and ate them all.

Just as quickly, he spat them out. "These are rabbit pellets!" he cried angrily.

"See?" Nanaboozhoo said. "You're smarter already."

Miigwech, Maya. My learning began in earnest with you.

There are no shortcuts to learning, and although I know I will forget to thank people, please know that I am grateful to you all for your patience with me as I learn the same things over and over. You relentlessly guide me away from smart berries and toward real learning. My life is better with you all in it.

Gary, my husband and partner, who provides a place of calm in the midst of my constant bouncing off in new directions: I love you forever. My boys, Ben, Max, and Sam, who took the best of me and improved on it: you are my heart, and I live vicariously through all the things that you do. Know that I've been trying to catch up with you from the moment you started to run. Angela and Charlie Minowe: you are joy to me. Welcome to the family. Much love to my parents who raised me; my father, who never forgot about me; and my grandparents, who shared their lives and stories with me. Thank you to Helen Wesley, my cousin who keeps the family tree and collects the stories of our far-flung family. To my cousin Joe Wesley and his mother, Romaine Lyon, for their time and teachings this past summer. I'll be back, and it won't take six years this time. To Josh Manitowabi, for his assistance with language. To Nancy Rowe, for her lodge and her teachings. The members of the Strong Water Women drum group: you are my spirit fire. Thank you to my sister-friends: Sabrina Shawana, Linda Hampton (Okie, MoonTree Woman), Shyann Jenkins, and Wanda Griffin. Celeste and Bruce Smith, thank you for conversations about land and your gracious hospitality. Next time we'll stay longer. Thank you to Jennifer Dock-stader, for welcoming me when I took my first tentative steps toward community. To Robyn Bourgeois, for listening and encouraging. To Karl Dockstader and Sean Vanderklis, for your friendship and having me back despite the mushroom suit thing. To Sherri Van-sickle, for showing up and inviting the drum group to teach your students: those early opportunities to speak and teach helped propel me here. To Neil Ellis Orts, for being brain to my heart and heart to my brain: you are a rare friend. To Kit Andres, for reminding me about things that are important and we'll have that mobile library one day; I just need to sell a couple more books. To Jane and Brian Andres: I am in awe of your ability to welcome and create family. Sara McGean and Twila Barnes: thank you for trusting me with your stories. To Kerry Goring, for years of friendship and conversation that have been nothing short of transformative. To Trish Heidebrecht Archibald, for helping me to start reading the biblical text differently. To Michael Krause, for conversations that have changed me and changed the book: I think the book is better because of your insights (at the very least, it is longer and my bookcase more crowded). To Jenessa Galenkamp, for welcome distractions and random questions. To Giniw Paradis for the beautiful beadwork that graces the cover and your years of friendship and teachings. I am so grateful. To Liz Lateef, for being my partner in disruption. To Nate Dirks, for creating a space to work through how our communities can become good relatives: your willingness and the work you are doing gave me hope when I needed it badly. Thank you to Darryl Leroux, for helping me understand how race shifting works and for being such a good example of claiming unwanted kin. To Harsha Walia, for friendship and solidarity: you help me connect with global themes and then make them intensely personal and real—much love xo. To Joy Henderson, Kelyn Best, Amber Starks, Azie Dungey, and Tiya Miles, for teaching me so much. Afro Indigenous people are real and part of our communities, and non-Black Natives have our own work to do in that regard. I have tried to remember each of you as I wrote this book. Thank you to Chanda Prescod-Weinstein, for reminding me to look up and challenging me when I don't think things completely through. To Rabbi Danya Ruttenberg, whose essays and Twitter threads have so often helped to reshape my perspective on old texts. Thank you to Daniel Heath Justice, for kindness, for being Thor to my Hulk, and for the reminder that sometimes, if we're very fortunate, we get to be Loki too. To Lee Francis IV, who, along with Daniel, reminds me to look for Indigenous people in the future. To Kaitlin Curtice, for helping me slow down and, along with Helen

Knott, for getting me past initial anxieties about this project: thank
you both. Alexis Shotwell: I love the way that you think, and you are
most welcome and wanted kin. To Rob Taylor Case, for misquoting
William Blake so beautifully I had to misquote you. Thank you to
Khadija Hammuda, for helping me connect our struggles: solidarity
and love to you. To Demita Frazier: you have a place in my heart,
and I will march beside you any day. And to Nick Estes, thank you
for your friendship and kindness and your beautiful words in the
foreward. Miigwech. To my editor, Valerie Weaver-Zercher: I have
appreciated your eye and your encouragement. Thank you for finding my writing and giving it a home.

To those who have been on the podcasts *Medicine for the Resistance* and *Aambe*, sometimes multiple times: I have appreciated your
time and the opportunity to learn. There are too many of you to list,
but know that I scroll through the episodes sometimes, marveling at
the people who have willingly shared knowledge and time with us.
The things you taught me are scattered through these pages.

To my reading posse: I have appreciated your feedback and comments. Every bit helped.

To the members of the Orphans of God Mailing List and the
NativeNet Bulletin Board: you were my earliest online communities.
Our parallel conversations about faith and being Indigenous set me
on a trajectory that brought me here, and I hold gratitude for and
fond memories of everyone I knew there. If I haven't already found
you on Facebook or Twitter, please find me. And all my tweeps who
have helped to shape my thinking and find better language for the
ideas in this book, thank you.

To the Board of the Fort Erie Friendship Center: it is an honor to
sit with each of you and do this work so that our community has a
place to come together. To the broader community around the Fort

Erie and Niagara Regional Native Centers: thank you so much for your welcome and kinship. For drumming and ceremony and celebration and a place to hold our collective joys and griefs. As Sabrina often says, there is unity in community.

And to those in my church, Chippewa Presbyterian: thank you for being part of my life. You are generous and hospitable to a fault.

Finally, to the land of the Ojibwe Anishinaabe that holds memory of me. To the waters that carried that knowledge to the place I live now, land that holds memory of Michi Saagiig Anishinaabe and Haudenosaunee. Land and water that remember treaties and agreements made between humans and greater-than-human relatives. Stars and other beings that bore witness to these agreements. I acknowledge and thank you for taking our follies and our gratitudes and still providing, still keeping your promises even while we don't keep ours. I say miigwech. Chi-miigwech. You are eternity in my hands, above my head, and beneath my feet.

# FURTHER READING

Augustine, Sarah. *The Land Is Not Empty.* Harrisonburg, VA: Herald Press, 2021.

Carlson-Manathara, Elizabeth, and Gladys Rowe. *Living in Indigenous Sovereignty.* Halifax: Fernwood Publishing, 2021.

Deer, Sarah. *The Beginning and End of Rape.* Minneapolis: University of Minnesota Press, 2015.

Dismantling the Doctrine of Discovery Coalition. *Stories of Repair: A Reparative Justice Resource toward Dismantling the Doctrine of Discovery.* 2021. Available for donation at dofdmenno.org.

Dunbar-Ortiz, Roxanne. *An Indigenous People's History of the United States.* Boston: Beacon Press, 2014.

Dunbar-Ortiz, Roxanne. *Not "A Nation of Immigrants": Settler Colonialism, White Supremacy, and a History of Erasure and Exclusion.* Boston: Beacon Press, 2021.

Estes, Nick. *Our History Is Our Future.* Brooklyn, NY: Verso, 2019.

Jennings, Willie James. *The Christian Imagination: Theology and the Origins of Race.* New Haven: Yale University, 2010.

Kaba, Mariame. *We Do This 'Til We Free Us.* Chicago: Haymarket Books, 2021.

Leroux, Darryl. *Distorted Descent: White Claims to Indigenous Identity.* Winnipeg: University of Manitoba Press, 2019.

Morales, Aurora Levins. *Medicine Stories: Essays for Radicals.* Durham: Duke University Press, 2019.

Mouallen, Omar. *Praying to the West: How Muslims Shaped the Americas.* Toronto: Simon & Schuster, 2021.

Norgaard, Kari Marie. *Salmon and Acorns Feed Our People.* New Brunswick, NJ: Rutgers University Press, 2019.

Prescod-Weinstein, Chanda. *The Disordered Cosmos.* New York: Bold Type Books, 2021.

Shotwell, Alexis. "Claiming Bad Kin." *Bearing* no. 3 (March 2019): 8–11.

Shotwell, Alexis. *Knowing Otherwise: Race, Gender, and Implicit Understanding.* University Park: Pennsylvania State University Press, 2011.

Simpson, Leanne Betasamosake. *As We Have Always Done.* Minneapolis: University of Minnesota Press, 2021.

Talaga, Tanya. *All Our Relations.* Toronto: House of Anansi Press, 2018.

Treuer, David. *The Heartbeat of Wounded Knee.* New York: Riverhead Books, 2019.

Walia, Harsha. *Border and Rule: Global Migration, Capitalism, and the Rise of Racist Nationalism.* Halifax, NS: Fernwood Publishing, 2021.

Wolfe, Patrick. *Traces of History: Elementary Structures of Race.* Brooklyn, NY: Verso, 2016.

# NOTES

## Introduction

11   *"When I say that the land":* Keolu Fox, "Rewriting Human History and Empowering Indigenous Communities with Genome Editing Tools," presentation at Center for Evolution and Medicine, Arizona State University, May 13, 2020. The video for this presentation is available at https://www.youtube.com/watch?v=vZw2TIBpBJs.

12   *"History is the story":* Aurora Levins Morales, *Medicine Stories: Essays for Radicals* (Durham, NC: Duke University Press, 2019), 71.

16   *"But as Patrick Wolfe":* Patrick Wolfe, "Settler Colonialism and the Elimination of the Native," *Journal of Genocide Research* 8, no. 4 (December 2006): 387–409.

17   *"Ultimately what we inherit":* Morales, *Medicine Stories*, 10.

17   *"To move those":* Alexis Shotwell, *Knowing Otherwise: Race, Gender, and Implicit Understanding* (Univesrity Park: Penn State University Press, 2011), 7–22.

22   *"Dr. Paulette Steeves talks about":* Paulette Steeves, *The Indigenous Paleolithic of the Western Hemisphere* (Lincoln: University of Nebraska, 2021), xxv.

## Chapter 1

25   *"When all of these":* Wendy Makoons Geniusz, *Our Knowledge Is Not Primitive: Decolonizing Botanical Anishinaabe Teachings* (Syracuse, NY: Syracuse University Press, 2009), 57.

27   *"I don't simply ask":* Steve Heinrichs, quoted in Elizabeth Carlson-Manathara and Gladys Rowe, *Living in Indigenous Sovereignty* (Halifax: Fernwood Publishing, 2021), 96.

32    *"As recently as 1912"*: Steeves, *The Indigenous Paleolithic*, 2.

32    *"Other oral histories"*: Steeves, *The Indigenous Paleolithic*, 10.

34    *"And human footprints"*: Scott Neuman, "Ancient Footprints Suggest
      Humans Lived in the Americas Earlier Than Once Thought," National
      Public Radio, *Science* (September 24, 2021), https://www.npr.org/2021
      /09/24/1040381802/ancient-footprints-new-mexico-white
      -sands-humans.

34    *"If animals like camels"*: Steeves, *The Indigenous Paleolithic*, 14.

37    *"Acosta developed"*: Willie James Jennings, *The Christian Imagination:
      Theology and the Origins of Race* (New Haven, CT: Yale University Press,
      2010), 98–115.

## Chapter 2

42    *"In her book All Our Relations"*: Tanya Talaga, *All Our Relations*
      (Toronto, ON: House of Anansi Press, 2018), 41.

44    *"Settler colonialism destroys"*: Wolfe, "Settler Colonialism and the
      Elimination of the Native."

44    *"Historian Roxanne Dunbar-Ortiz"*: Roxanne Dunbar-Ortiz, *Not
      "A Nation of Immigrants": Settler Colonialism, White Supremacy, and a
      History of Erasure and Exclusion* (Boston: Beacon Press, 2021), 157.

51    *"In the 1823 ruling"*: Sara Augustine, *The Land Is Not Empty*
      (Harrisonburg, VA: Herald Press, 2021), 90.

53    *"The Doctrine of Discovery"*: Augustine, *The Land Is Not Empty*, 28.

## Chapter 3

59    *"There is no such thing"*: Patrick Wolfe, *Traces of History: Elementary
      Structures of Race* (Brooklyn, NY: Verso, 2016), 23.

60    *"In his book Praying to the West"*: Omar Mouallem, *Praying to the West:
      How Muslims Shaped the Americas* (Toronto: Simon & Schuster, 2021),
      186.

60    *"A primarily African labor force"*: Mouallem, *Praying to the West*, 58.

67    *"There was, he said"*: Roxanne Dunbar-Ortiz, *An Indigenous People's
      History* (Boston: Beacon Press, 2014), 158.

70    *"In Traces of History"*: Wolfe, *Traces of History*, 25.

## Chapter 4

81    *"In fact, just five white people"*: Antonio Moore, "Who Owns Almost All America's Land?" Inequality.org, February 15, 2016, https://inequality.org/research/owns-land/.

81    *"There are about fifty-five"*: Joe Mitchell, "Forest Service National Resource Guide to American Indian and Alaska Native Relations," December 5, 1997. Appendix D, https://www.fs.fed.us/people/tribal/tribexd.pdf.

82    *"The UN Genocide Convention"*: *Convention on the Prevention and Punishment of the Crime of Genocide, Article 2*, http://www.hrweb.org/legal/genocide.html.

88    *"Illnesses like smallpox"*: Patrick J. Kiger, "Did Colonists Give Infected Blankets to Native Americans," History.com, November 25, 2019, https://www.history.com/news/colonists-native-americans-smallpox-blankets.

89    *"Describing this in his book"*: David Treuer, *The Heartbeat of Wounded Knee* (New York: Riverhead Books, 2019), 93.

90    *"In his book Our History Is the Future"*: Nick Estes, *Our History Is Our Future* (Brooklyn, NY: Verso Estes, 2019), 124.

93    *"made of ticky tacky"*: Reference to the Pete Seeger song "Little Boxes."

97    *"The 1978 Indian Child Welfare Act"*: Ruth Hopkins, "How Foster Care Has Stripped Native American Children of Their Own Cultures," *Teen Vogue,* May 22, 2018, https://www.teenvogue.com/story/foster-care-has-failed-native-american-youth.

97    *"Canadian numbers"*: Reducing the number of Indigenous children in care 2021.

99    *"The amount, twenty-one billion"*: Dan Sperling, "In 1825, Haiti Paid France 21 Billion to Preserve Its Independence—Time For France to Pay It Back." December 6, 2017, https://www.forbes.com/sites/realspin/2017/12/06/in-1825-haiti-gained-independence-from-france-for-21-billion-its-time-for-france-to-pay-it-back/?sh=35a47052312b.

## Chapter 5

104    *"Based on the Calvinist idea"*: Mariame Kaba, *We Do This til We Free Us* (Chicago: Haymarket Books, 2021), 73.

105 *"With this new space"*: Kaba, *We Do This til We Free Us*, 72, 111.

105 *"In We Do This"*: Kaba, *We Do This til We Free Us*, 21.

106 *"In the United States"*: Roxanne Daniel, "Since You Asked: What Data Exists about Native American People in the Criminal Justice System?" April 22, 2020, https://www.prisonpolicy.org/blog/2020/04/22/native/.

106 *"For every one hundred"*: US incarceration rates by race and ethnicity, 2010, https://www.prisonpolicy.org/graphs/raceinc.html.

106 *"Indigenous women account for"*: Government of Canada, "Indigenous People in Federal Custody Surpasses 30%," January 21, 2020, https://www.oci-bec.gc.ca/cnt/comm/press/press20200121-eng.aspx.Canada 2020.

108 *"We also know that women"*: David W. Anthony, *The Horse, the Wheel, and Language: How Bronze-Age Riders from Eurasian Steppes Shaped the Modern World* (Princeton: Princeton University Press, 2010), 153.

109 *"The homicide rate"*: Sarah Deer, *The Beginning and End of Rape* (Minneapolis: University of Minnesota Press, 2015), 4–6.

110 *"This actually has real life"*: Naomi Ishisaka, "Contrasting Coverage of Gabby Petito Case and Missing and Murdered Indigenous People Shows 'Absolute Injustice,'" September 27, 2021, https://www.seattletimes.com/seattle-news/contrasting-coverage-of-gabby-petito-case-and-missing-and-murdered-indigenous-people-shows-absolute-injustice/.

112 *"She notes that"*: Barbara Gurr, *Reproductive Justice* (New Brunswick, NJ: Rutgers University Press, 2015), 125.

115 *"The report documents"*: Inquiry Comissioners, "Reclaiming Power and Space: The Final Report of the National Inquiry into Missing and Murdered Indigenous Women and Girls," Canada, 2019, https://www.mmiwg-ffada.ca/final-report/. Inquiry Comissioners, 258.

116 *"Rape embodies the worst"*: Deer, *The Beginning*, 51.

118 *"In November 2021"*: Associated Press, "102 Died at Native American Boarding School in Nebraska," November 13, 2021, https://www.usnews.com/news/best-states/nebraska/articles/2021-11-13/102-died-at-native-american-board-school-in-nebraska?src=usn_tw.

## Chapter 6

123  *"In the Anishinaabe universe"*: Louise Erdrich, *Books and Islands in Ojibwe Country* (New York: Harper Perennial, 2014), 72.

124  *"In his book Anishinaabe Ways"*: Lawrence Gross, *Anishinaabe Ways of Knowing and Being* (New York: Ashgate Publishing, 2014), 104.

125  *"In her book The Hebrew Bible"*: Mari Joerstad, *The Hebrew Bible and Environmental Ethics* (Cambridge: Cambridge University Press, 2019), 11.

125  *"Joerstad draws together"*: Joerstad, *The Hebrew Bible*, 9.

131  *"The Karuk people"*: Kari Marie Norgaard, *Salmon and Acorns Feed Our People* (New Brunswick: Rutgers University Press, 2019), 9, 19, 21.

132  *"Those early Israelites"*: Exodus 34:13.

133  *"He sold it to them"*: Katrina Phillips, "When Grandma Went to Washington: Ojibwe Activism and the Battle over the Apostle Islands Lakeshore," *Journal of Native American and Indigenous Studies Association* 8, no. 2 (2021): 29–61.

133  *"In the May 2021 issue"*: David Treuer, "Return the National Parks to the Tribes," *The Atlantic*, April 12, 2021, https://www.theatlantic.com/magazine/archive/2021/05/return-the-national-parks-to-the-tribes/618395/.

135  *"You'll have to get off"*: John Steinbeck, *Grapes of Wrath* (New York: Viking Press, 1939), 34, 35.

136  *"In The Indigenous Paleolithic"*: Steeves, *The Indigenous Paleolithic*, 166.

137  *"Inuk singer"*: Tanya Tagaq, Twitter post January 10, 2022, 10:49 am, https://twitter.com/tagaq/status/1480567495538970627?s=20.

138  *"Human action has caused"*: Joerstad, *The Hebrew Bible*, 143, emphasis mine.

139  *"There was a time"*: Erdrich, *Books and Islands*, 16.

140  *"Second, as Willie James Jennings"*: Jennings, *The Christian Imagination*, 255.

141  *"As Eve Tuck"*: Eve Tuck, [info], 2012.

141  *"In Salmon and Acorns"*: Norgaard, *Salmon and Acorns*, 32.

142  *"The desert"*: Isaiah 35:1.

## Chapter 7

147   *"Naomi Klein has said"*: Carlson-Manathara and Rowe, *Living in Indigenous Sovereignty*, 15.

151   *"In her book As We Have Always Done"*: Leanne Betasamosake Simpson, *As We Have Always Done* (Minneapolis: University of Minnesota Press, 2021), 8.

153   *"In Not "A Nation of Immigrants""*: Dunbar-Ortiz, *Not "A Nation of Immigrants,"* 45–46.

153   *"She contrasts"*: Dunbar-Ortiz, *Not "A Nation of Immigrants,"* 47–49.

154   *"But the tests are flawed"*: Kim Tallbear, *Native American DNA: Tribal Belonging and the False Promise of Genetic Science* (Minneapolis: University of Minnesota Press, 2013), 6.

156   *"Matt, a white Twitter user"*: Twitter user Matt, @witch_of_SoCo Twitter Post. May 4, 2021, 4:57 pm, https://twitter.com/Witch_of_So Co/status/1389685525888442368?s=20.

159   *"Sarah Ahmed writes"*: Sara Ahmed, *Living a Feminist Life* (Durham, NC: Duke University Press, 2017), 117.

163   *"In her essay"*: Alexis Shotwell, "Claiming Bad Kin," *Bearing* (March 2019): 8–11.

164   *"All of us inherit"*: Shotwell, "Claiming Bad Kin."

164   *"In her essay"*: Alexis Levins Morales, *Medicine Stories* (Durham, NC: Duke University Press, 2019), 101.

167   *"In Our Knowledge"*: Geniusz, *Our Knowledge*, 81, 82.

## Chapter 8

174   *"Many of the settler Canadians"*: Carlson-Manathara and Rowe, *Living in Indigenous Sovereignty*, 193.

175   *"In the chapter on spiritual growth"*: Gross, *Anishinaabe Ways*, 235–237.

178   *"There is always possibility"*: Gross, *Anishinaabe Ways*, 112.

179   *"In her book"*: Augustine, *The Land Is Not Empty*, 169.

180   *"Land theft includes"*: Norgaard, *Salmon and Acorns*, 78.

180   *"Indigenous peoples globally"*: Hannah Rundel, "Indigenous Knowledge Can Help Solve the Biodiversity Crisis," *Scientific American*,

October 12, https://blogs.scientificamerican.com/observations/indigenous
-knowledge-can-help-solve-the-biodiversity-crisis/.

180 *"Once we understand"*: Rundel, "Indigenous Knowledge," 213.

182 *"In the foreword of"*: Carlson-Manathara and Rowe, *Living in Indigenous Sovereignty*, 2.

183 *"In Praying to the West"*: Moulland, *Praying to the West*, 290.